CHARLES DE FOUCAULD
In the Footsteps of Jesus of Nazareth

CHARLES DE FOUCAULD
In the Footsteps of Jesus of Nazareth

by
Little Sister Annie of Jesus

New City

London

First published in France
as
Charles de Foucauld.. Sur les pas de Jésus de Nazareth
by
Nouvelle Cité
© archives générales des Petites Soeurs de Jésus
© Novelle Cité 2001

First Published in English
by
New City
Unit 17, Sovereign Park,
Coronation Road, London NW10 7QP

Translated by the Little Sisters of Jesus
© English Translation 2004 the Little Sisters of Jesus
©All pictures: Archive of the Little Sisters of Jesus, Rome

Cover design by Tomeu Mayans

British Cataloguing-in-Publication Data
A catalogue record for this book is available
from the British Library

ISBN 0 904287 90 4

Typeset by New City, London

Printed and bound by The Cromwell Press,
Trowbridge, Wiltshire

CONTENTS

In the Footsteps of Jesus of Nazareth

PREFACE

Charles de Foucauld was born in the mid-19th century into an old aristocratic French family. He spent the key years of his life in the Sahara desert as a Christian 'monk' among the local Tuareg people, who were followers of Islam. There he met his death in 1916, in the central Saharan oasis of Tamanrasset.

What, we can well ask, has he to say to us? We live in a world far removed from his, and our personal lives, whatever they may be, are surely quite unlike his. And yet, surprisingly, his life has had a profound influence on many today. People of all kinds have discovered through him 'a word of life' that gives meaning to their everyday lives, and a little sign of hope to encourage them on their journey.

The French society in which Charles was born and grew up was marked by strong, and often bitter, class distinctions. In theory the French Revolution, with its famous slogan of 'Liberté, Egalité, Fraternité' (derived from the United States' Independence struggle), had abolished these distinctions. In fact the old feudal order, with its clear social hierarchy and its integration of Church and State, was replaced by new class divisions linked to the industrial revolution. The old feudal loyalties were replaced by the harsh economic laws of 'hire and fire': the worker became a 'hired hand', to be employed or laid aside, as needed.

This social context helps us to grasp the radical nature of Charles' desire to imitate Jesus as the 'workman of Nazareth'. Was not Jesus the 'carpenter'? This, Charles reminds us, is a truth we had largely forgotten! And had he not chosen to be at the bottom of the social ladder, in 'the lowest place'?

Accompanying this industrialization, the western European powers engaged in a massive colonial expansion, especially in Africa. This led, inevitably, to an open or latent hostility between the new 'rulers', the colonizing military and civil authorities, and the 'ruled', the local peoples. It was in this situation that Charles wished to be 'the universal brother', a brother to each and every person he encountered. Such a simple and bold claim strikes at the heart of inhuman structures and relationships, and begins to remake a world of respect and equality. Charles did this, not by words – he, as we do, mistrusted mere words – but by simple, everyday actions and gestures, with a readiness, when need be, to denounce abuses and take risks.

Work, especially manual work, was also looked down on by the Tuareg nobles. While few of us realize that the Sahara is even inhabited, the Tuareg, with whom Charles lived for over ten years, were a large but scattered group of nomadic peoples in the central Sahara, with an elaborate class structure. They have a rich and ancient culture and a deep faith, that of Islam. As Charles came to realize by sharing their life and studying their culture in detail, they looked down on the French occupants as 'pagans' and as 'barbarians'. (Most of the French, even if nominally Christian, did not express or practise their faith.) The Tuareg saw them as people with superior force of arms and material, technological means but with no sense of authentic values such as hospitality, freedom and courage.

Reading Charles' letters and personal reflections, we discover his own struggles to 'see through' the ingrained, largely unconscious opinions of national and religious superiority, and to begin to see the different, but equally real worth of the 'other.' As the French settlers came to bring 'civilization' and 'Christianity', so perhaps we in today's West are tempted as neo-colonialists to offer, even impose, 'free trade and democracy' as well as our modern religion of 'secular humanism'. Let us allow Charles to challenge us! How sadly we deform the real values and truths that are ours, and close ourselves to the truth and goodness of those different from ourselves!

It is perhaps fortunate that Charles lost his Christian faith in adolescence. By rediscovering it through the living example of his Muslim hosts (in Morocco especially), he was not tempted to despise the profound value of their religion, or its providential role in God's plan. Returning to his Christian faith as a mature adult, he never doubted its God-given and absolute truth and he built his whole life, without reserve, around it. The lived example of Brother Charles – totally faithful to Jesus, totally respectful of God's ways in his neighbours – is surely a light for us today, particularly in relation to Islam and the Muslim people.

Charles as an adult had little, in fact almost no, experience of the ordinary life of the French Church of his day. Soon after his discovery of faith he became a monk and left for a poor monastery in Syria. But the religious picture in France was a complicated one. There were the 'Jansenists', who over-emphasized the judgment of God and the demand for ever stricter moral standards. There were the 'Modernists', who over emphasized the application of human reason, tending to interpret religion in terms of our developing human history and psychology. And then there were the 'Sceptics', those who denied the truth of any religious belief. Those who remained in the Church were influenced by their criticisms and doubts, not unlike us in our own day. While these factors had played a role in Charles' loss of faith as an adolescent, it seems as though once he found a genuine adult faith, he never allowed himself to be pulled into factional disputes but went to the 'centre' of faith, the person of Jesus. He went always to the 'heart of the matter', the unfathomable love of the one Source of all in the human life of Jesus, the man of Nazareth.

It must be added that the Catholic Church in France was also under attack at this time from the secular society. Many of its institutions had been closed, properties seized and most religious orders were disbanded. The very presence of missionaries in the colonies was barely tolerated. This had an important effect on the ability of the Church to confront certain social structures both at home and abroad, not the least of which was the question of slavery. Although Charles' military connections, as a former French officer and explorer, gave him a certain privileged access to the Saharan territories, he refused to be a 'dumb sentinel' but protested with vigour against the institution and practice of slavery.

On his return from exploring the interior of Morocco Charles wrote a book which became a best seller. If then he was known in his day as an 'explorer', we can also see that his whole life was an 'exploration'. Having discovered Jesus, he sought to discover who this Jesus really was. Visiting the little town of Nazareth, he suddenly became aware that Jesus had lived and worked in this ordinary, out-of-the-way place as a manual worker for some thirty years, in fact for all but three years of his life. If God became 'one of us', as he firmly believed, was it not extraordinary that God had chosen to enter our human history in this apparently 'insignificant' way? A way that is 'our' way: the way that most of us live, the way of our common experience...

Charles explored and developed this insight for the rest of his life. It is the hidden 'key' that opens the door to our understanding of Charles' life, and to the interest and importance of the 'message' that his life may have for each of us.

We can easily be absorbed by the dramatic and picturesque life of Charles as the intrepid explorer, risking his life, and then as the solitary 'hermit in the Sahara'. During this time of exploration he already wanted to get to know, understand and to be with the local people. On his return as a priest, he sought to found a 'fraternity', a community of brothers who would live his ideal of universal brotherhood. His conception of being a brother to one and all was not just a human ideal, but the lived consequence of Charles' deep belief that God had come to share our life and to live as one of us, to be 'our Brother'.

Our faith is so often separate from our daily life and choices. For Charles, to follow Jesus was to become 'like Jesus', and to act like Jesus with every person and in every situation.

Of course we don't, most of us, live in the desert! Nor do we live in Charles' world or share his limited need of food and sleep, nor his almost boundless energy. But through him we can, each of us, whatever our situation, find inspiration – a 'breath of the Spirit', through him for our often empty lives.

This little book gives us all the material we need to get in touch with the inner workings of Brother Charles' life and, through him, with the living presence of Jesus, his constant Companion and Friend.

Ian Lathan
Little Brother of Jesus

INTRODUCTION

Charles de Foucauld was born in Strasbourg in 1858. The early loss of both father and mother, at the age of six, left a deep scar in the young child.

During a difficult adolescence, he lost his faith and, perhaps to compensate for the profound sadness that he bore in his heart, he plunged into a life of pleasure and disorder.

As a young army officer, aged twenty-two, he was sent to Algeria. Two years later, he left the army and undertook a risky exploration in Morocco. The witness of the Muslim faith awakened in him the question: "Does God exist?"

On his return to France, touched by the affectionate and discreet welcome of his deeply Christian family, he began to search for the truth, and he met, providentially, a priest who became for him a father and a friend: Abbé Huvelin. In October 1886 at the age of 28, he converted.

From this moment, he wanted to give his whole life to God. A pilgrimage in the Holy Land revealed to him the figure of Jesus of Nazareth: a figure that fascinated him, a figure he will follow and imitate. He spent, first of all, seven years in a Trappist monastery, and then four years in Nazareth, as a hermit at the door of a Poor Clare convent. Progressively, he discovered that to follow Jesus and to love him passionately involved coming close to those who are far off, those who are "most abandoned".

Ordained priest in 1901, he left for the Sahara, settling first at Beni Abbès and then at Tamanrasset, with the aim simply of becoming the friend and brother of the desert nomads, through learning their language and entering into their culture. He did not seek to convert but to love, wishing to "cry the Gospel" throughout the whole of his life.

On 1 December 1916, in the Hoggar (central Sahara), he died, assassinated. It was during the First World War, and he had chosen to remain to the end among his friends.

There are many biographies about this man of God who has marked out, for thousands of disciples, an authentic Gospel way.

This book, made up of extracts from his writings, is a little initiation into his spirituality. Its aim is simply to give the reader a taste to go further and to discover more of 'Brother Charles of Jesus', as he came to call himself.

As he wrote to one of his childhood friends: "Imitation is inseparable from love: it's the secret of my life. I've lost my heart for this Jesus of Nazareth, crucified one thousand nine hundred years ago, and I spend my life trying to imitate Him, as best as my weakness allows."*

* Lettres à un ami de lycée, Nouvelle Cite, p. 159. [Letters to a School Friend]

No one who begins to listen to Brother Charles can remain indifferent, for his life and writings bring us back again and again to the living Person of Jesus and to His message.

He will, I hope, draw us too along the steps of this Jesus of Nazareth, his "Beloved Brother and Lord".

Little Sister Annie of Jesus

I

THE YEARS OF UNBELIEF
AND THE PATH TO CONVERSION

Childhood and Teenage Years

Charles de Foucauld was born on 15 September 1858, in Strasbourg, which is located in the Province of Alsace on the border between France and Germany. Twelve years later Alsace would be annexed to Germany as a prize in the War of 1870.

Charles' family was a rich one and belonged to the aristocracy. His family had a longstanding military tradition.

When Charles reminisced about his childhood, he rarely mentioned his father, an inspector of forests and waterways who lived away from the family because he was quite ill. But he would often speak with emotion of the tender affection and the piety of his mother.

> *From babyhood I was surrounded by so many graces, son of a holy mother, who taught me to know you, to love you and to pray to you as soon as I could babble.*
>
> *La Derniere place,* p. 100

Charles at about 4 years of age, with his mother and little sister.

But he was not to enjoy this maternal presence for long. Very early, tragedy struck his life, and the little six-year-old boy lost both his mother and his father within the space of a few months. The wound was deep and lasting.

Charles' maternal grandfather took him under his care. A few years later, he experienced a new grief: he had to flee before the German invasion when war broke out between France and Germany in 1870, for Strasbourg was close to the border. After France's defeat, Charles' grandfather chose to settle in Nancy, which was in the part of the neighbouring province of Lorraine that had remained French.

At the age of twelve, Charles was already an orphan and a refugee. These deep losses left him with painful feelings of inner emptiness. We see him on the threshold of adolescence as a child who kept to himself, an uncommunicative, sensitive, troubled boy.

He had an intelligent, inquiring mind and developed an early passion for reading. The historical period in which he grew up was marked by religious scepticism and philosphies that accepted only scientific facts as truth. People believed that science alone could find the answers to the great questions of human existence. Before long Charles had lost his faith. He said himself that he was an unbeliever for twelve years.

By the time I was 15 or 16 I had no trace of faith left. The books I used to devour had done this to me. I didn't subscribe to any specific philosophy,

23

Charles, aged 18, on his entry to Saint-Cyr.

as none of them seemed solidly proved enough to me. I doubted everything, especially the Catholic faith, since there were several of its dogmas that I found insulting to reason.
Letter to H. Duveyrier, 21 Feb. 1892

More or less unconsciously he was searching for a true reason to live. He rather reminds us of many young people today who despair of finding a deep meaning to life.

Later he wrote to his cousin about this period of his life:

I was nothing but selfishness, irreverence, immorality. I went wild.
Letters to Mme. de Bondy, 17 April 1892

His letters to his childhood friend, Gabriel Tourdes, show an extreme need for immediate gratification, a kind of frenzy for life, as if perhaps to get rid of the agonising distress he felt inside.

Dear old Tourdes, it's been a long time since I wrote to you. I'm coming on Friday. I want to warn you I'll be counting on you every night. We'll go back to our reading with a rage. I'm furiously happy about coming back to Nancy for a while. I'm planning to enjoy myself completely, body and mind.
Lettres à un Ami de Lycée, p. 49

25

He was 20 when he finished his officer's training at the military school of St. Cyr, but his military career was only to last three years.

His grandfather had just died. The great effect it had on him shows how deeply sensitive he was.

> *At Nancy an immense sorrow befell me. I lost my grandfather. I admired his high intelligence, and his inexhaustible affection had enfolded my youth and childhood in an atmosphere of love. I can still feel the warmth of it and it always moves me. His death hurt me terribly, and fourteen years later [it was 3 February 1878 that he died] the pain is still sharp.*
>
> Letter to H. Duvreyier, 21 Feb. 1892

From that time on nothing held him back. To make up for the emptiness in his heart, he threw himself into a life of worldly pleasure, which was all the easier for him to do as he had a great deal of money.

> *I fell into a disorderly life and lived that way a long time, though it didn't kill off my fondness for study. In the regiment I ran wild, since none of my family were around. I saw scarcely anyone from my family between 1878 and 1886. What little they knew of my life, especially at the beginning of those years, can only have distressed them.*
>
> From the same letter

After his conversion, Brother Charles looked at this part of his life again, under the light of faith. His aim was not to dwell on the past but to sing a kind of hymn to God's mercy.

With a sense of wonder he discovered that when he had been straying far from God, refusing to believe in him, when he had been sunk in sin, God had always been there waiting for him, seeking him, guiding him with infinite love, though he did not know it.

> *I was going further and further from you, my Lord and my Life. And so my life was turning into death. And in this state of death, you still watched over me. You made me feel a painful emptiness, a sadness the like of which I've never felt before or since. It came over me every night when I went home to my lodgings. What we called our festivities left me silent and heavy-hearted. You gave me the vague restlessness of a troubled conscience, for though my conscience was asleep it was not altogether dead. I have never felt that sadness, that ill ease, that restlessness at any time but then. It must have been your gift, my God. I was far from suspecting this. How good you are! How you kept me safe! How you sheltered me under your wings when I didn't even believe you existed!*
> *La Derniere place,* pp. 101-102

Brother Charles' own painful experience of sin led him to the conviction that God loves people unconditionally with a love that is altogether freely given. And because God's love for each of his creatures is so passionate, God had never stopped waiting for him, seeking him, looking after him all the years he was astray.

> *My God, how good you are! At the very moment when you punished Adam, you offered him hope, the hope of the greatest glory and the greatest happiness. You let him see from afar the "seed" and the blessed woman by whom the serpent's head would be crushed. How good you are, my God, and how unchanging, you who do not break the crushed reed or quench the wavering flame.*
>
> *And isn't this exactly what you still do every day? Don't you call to us by the voice of your Church and tell us that whatever our sins, however long our unfaithfulness has lasted, we need only return to you and repent and we will be saved. You will not only deliver us from every evil but make us heirs to all glory and all happiness. No sinner is so great, no wrong-doer so hardened, but you will offer him Paradise at the top of your voice, as you did to the good thief in response to a mere moment's good will.*
>
> *Qui peut resister à Dieu*, p. 30-31

Doesn't Brother Charles' conviction have something to say to us today? People so often talk about the absence of God. Is not the place where things seem most to tell us God is absent precisely the place where God is? Doesn't God remain mysteriously present in the hearts of those who reject him, as he does in those who worship him?

This is what the great prophets of the Old Testament were talking about: "Does a woman forget her baby at the breast or fail to cherish the child of her womb? Yet even if these forget, I will never forget you. I have branded you on the palms of my hands." [Is 49:15-16]

How are we to answer for our faith today except to bear witness to it right in the deserts of the world? By our whole lives we bear witness to the unfathomable love of God for every human being, especially for those whom the world abandons, excludes, gives up on.

The Path to Conversion

As the nineteenth century drew to a close, France was carving out a vast colonial empire for itself in Africa and Asia.

In 1830, France began a war for the conquest of Algeria. After gradually occupying and annexing the whole territory, the French army stayed on and was in charge of the administration of the southern territories, including the Saharan oases.

Thus it was that in 1881Charles, a young officer of 23, was sent to Algeria to the garrison of Setif. He arrived accompanied by a young lady he had taken up with, and tried at first to pass her off as his wife. His commanding officers gave him the order several times to break off with her. He refused and the punishment fell: *"Removed from active duty for indiscipline augmented by notorious misconduct."*

Overnight he was back in France.

Why this impulsive response? It doesn't seem to have been because of how attached he was to the young woman, for he left her just as abruptly a few months later. But he was fiercely independent and couldn't bear to have his freedom interfered with. Nobody had the right to make him give in.

A few weeks later as he was whiling away his time at a large hotel in Evian, he learned that his regiment was taking part in opertaions in Tunisia. Instantly he applied to be reinstated into the army and was accepted, but in another regiment in Southern Algeria where there had been an uprising.

Why this turnaround? A taste for adventure and danger was probably the chief factor, as is shown in this letter to G. Tourdes:

> *An expedition like this is too rare a pleasure.*
> *I can't let it go by without trying to get in on the fun.*
> *Lettre à un Ami de Lycée,* p. 116

But wasn't something else involved, less consciously perhaps: an upsurge of generosity, a feeling of solidarity?

Charles, aged 20, a sub lieutenant in the cavalry.

What lets us think this is that as soon as he got there to take part in the expedition he showed himself *"just as able to put up with privation and fatigue as he had put up with pleasure. Unfailingly in good spirits, he bore hunger and even thirst cheerfully. He was good to his men, always looking for ways to make things better for them and sharing their lot completely."*

Lesourd, La Vraie figure du P. de Foucauld, p. 62
based on the testimony of FitzJames

The vast spaces of southern Algeria fascinated Charles de Foucauld. He fell in love with Africa.

Once again, a few months later, he quit the army. This time it was for good. But now he did it to stay where he was and start carefully getting ready to explore Morocco.

He made his trip with a learned Jewish Rabbi, Mardochee, under a false identity as a fellow Rabbi. It led him into many dangers, since the Kingdom of Morocco was a closed country and Europeans were forbidden to enter it.

He had gone to Algeria as one of the powerful, a member of a conquering army. The only way he could enter Morocco was as one of the poor, disguised as an outcast Jew.

For nearly a year, from June 1883 to May 1884, he was in severe conditions of poverty and social stigma, things he had never experienced before. His friend the explorer Duvreyier later said that during his trip Charles *"made a vow of poverty and destitution, and more than kept it."*

It was an experience he would never forget.

As he went along sharing the life of the Jewish communities who gave him hospitality, he took part in their Sabbath prayers.

Travelling without defence in a strange land, he could have been killed at any moment and was totally dependent on those who took him under their roof. Twice his Muslim or Jewish hosts saw through his disguise. If he came out alive it was because they were believers and held the life of a guest sacred. Charles never forgot these heights of hospitality.

He saw Muslims at their daily prayers, and their testimony of prayer affected him:

> *Islam made a very deep impression on me. The sight of such faith, of people living continually in the presence of God, made me glimpse something greater and truer than worldly pursuits. I set about studying Islam, and then the Bible.*
>
> Letter to H. de Castries, 8 July 1901

It was not Christians, then, who woke up Charles' religious yearnings. Rather, it was other believers, they too children of Abraham. God alone holds the secret of such mysterious connections.

Charles stayed in Algiers during 1885, writing up his travel notes. He had frequent contacts with Commandant Titre, a geographer whose daughter,

Charles, aged 25, before going to Morocco.

Marguerite, was 23. An affection soon sprang up between Charles and Marguerite, and in May 1885, they decided to get engaged. Charles wrote to her:

> *I shall leave you free to do as you like in religious matters, but as for myself I shan't go to church, as I do not have the faith.*
> *Cahiers Ch. de Foucauld 25,* p. 38

At the end of May Charles went back to France and found his family dead set against the engagement. A few months later he decided to break it off. Doing it cost him a lot, especially, so it seems, at the thought of the pain he was imposing on the young woman, who was very fond of him.

His trip through Morocco had left him a far more mature person, and had made him a famous man.

His family welcomed him warmly. What touched him deeply was that they made no moralistic allusions to his stormy past. They just expressed their joy at having him back again. This reception had something in it that already reminds us of the parable of the prodigal son.

The ones who welcomed him most were his sister and his cousin Marie. They were Christians and didn't hide the fact. They asked Charles no questions, but he felt stirrings of his own.

> *When I was in Paris, I found myself among people who were very intelligent, very virtuous and*

deeply Christian. I told myself that this religion
might not be so absurd after all.
Letres à Henry de Castries, 14 Aug 1901, p. 95

The watchful, unobtrusive presence of his cousin, Marie de Bondy, for whom Charles kept a deep bond of affection all his life, touched him greatly. He was grateful most of all for her discretion:

> *She seconded your work, my God, by her*
> *silence, her gentleness and her goodness. She*
> *was kind, but she didn't intervene.*
> *La Derniere place,* p. 105

The Return of the Prodigal

The young explorer was searching. He was indifferent to the glowing praises the Geographical Society gave him for his work in Morocco. His attention was elsewhere now. His unbelief had yielded to uncertainty and he began sincerely searching for the truth.

He started by immersing himself in classical philosophy, but became disenchanted. He then began reading a book by Bossuet, "Elévations sur les Mystères," which his cousin Marie de Bondy had given him. It was a commentary on the Gospel of John. Through this reading he began to realize that it was impossible to reach God through his own will power, for God is not an idea to master but a person to encounter.

And so, like someone groping in the dark, he went looking for that encounter and set his heart on it. This was the turning point he would call "the dawn of my conversion" in a meditation on the parable of the prodigal son.

> *Your first grace, the one I see as the dawn of my conversion, was to have given me a hunger. It was then I came back to you, timidly groping my way, and repeating this strange prayer: "If you exist, then let me know you."*
>
> On Lk 15:11-32, *from L'Imitation du Bien-aimé,* pp.78-79

The lost son at last had heard the Father's call that echoes through the centuries, ever since Genesis: "Adam, where are you?"

The months went by. Into the story came the one who would be the instrument of Charles' encounter with God, Father Huvelin. [To learn more about Fr. Huvelin, see *Un Précurseur, l'Abbé Huvelin*, by L. Portier.]

This priest, trained as a historian and a specialist in classical Greek, had chosen to remain a humble curate at the church of St. Augustine in Paris, refusing any higher post. For 35 years he exercised his apostolate as a priest.

His health was fragile and he had an extreme sensitivity to the suffering of others. He welcomed, comforted and transformed many penitents. Crowds flocked to hear his sermons.

Well aware of the modernist controversy that was dividing the French Church, he took no part in it. He was simply the friend and confidant of those who found themselves torn between their deepest convictions and some of the Church's decisions.

Marie de Bondy was one of Fr. Huvelin's parishioners and had spoken about him to her cousin. Charles later wrote:

> *Lord, when you made me enter his confessional on one of the last days in October 1886, you gave me everything. If there is joy in heaven when a sinner repents, then there must have been some when I entered that confessional. I asked for religious instruction. He told me to kneel down and make my confession.*
>
> *La Derniere place,* p. 106

Point blank, Fr. Huvelin answered this young man he barely knew, and who was asking to discuss religion with him, by an invitation to conversion: bring the truth into your inmost heart by acknowledging yourself as a sinner and "come to the light".

Only when our hearts are broken in sorrow for our sins can God make them new again as "hearts of flesh."

Charles hesitated a moment at the invitation. Then without arguing he obeyed. The man who had never accepted to bend his will to someone else knelt down, acknowledged his faults and experienced an inexpressible joy, the joy of the prodigal son. He recalled that moment ten years later, writing at Nazareth:

> *How good the prodigal son's father is. But you were a thousand times more generous than he. You did a thousand times more for me than he for his son. How good you are my Lord and my God! When I was that prodigal son, I was not just welcomed with unspeakable kindness and without punishment, without reprimand, with no reminders of the past. I was not just welcomed with kisses, with the finest robe and a signet ring as a child of the house. Not just all that, but my blessed Father came looking for me and brought me back from the faraway country.*
>
> L'imitation du Bien-aimé, p. 79

In the same text he speaks of the Eucharist:

> *And how divine was the banquet you have invited me to, so much beyond the banquet for the prodigal son. You brought me in to that banquet immediately.*
>
> L'imitation du Bien-aimé, p. 79

Charles was conscious of being poor and a sinner. It was in this frame of mind that he met the God of Love, who forgives without limit, who is always out looking for the lost sheep. And under the sign of broken bread, he already had a glimpse of the one who came as a poor man to encounter our human race, and who is always there among us walking with us.

Charles had found his faith, but as he himself admitted:

> *At the beginning, this faith of mine had many obstacles to overcome. I had doubted for so long, I didn't believe everything in a day. Sometimes it was the miracles in the Gospels I found unbelievable, sometimes I wanted to mix passages from the Koran in with my prayers. But divine grace and the advice of my confessor blew the fog away.*
> Letter to H. de Castries, 14 August 1901

Before long, he would experience something like what St. Paul meant when he wrote to the Corinthians: *"If anyone is in Christ, he is a new creation." [2 Cor 5:17]*

A few years later Charles wrote:

> *It is so true that the just live by faith, for faith replaces most of our natural senses. Through our senses we perceive nothing but deceptive appearances; sight shows us a poor person; faith shows us Jesus. The ear makes us hear insults and threats; faith sings to us, "rejoice and be glad". Touch makes us feel rocks thrown at us; faith tells us, "Be glad you have had the honour of suffering something for Christ's name." Taste tells us it is a little unleavened*

40

bread; faith shows us "Jesus the Saviour". Our senses love wealth and prestige; faith detests them: "What people think highly of is loathsome in the sight of God"... "Happy are the poor". And faith reveres the poverty and the lowliness in which Jesus clothed his whole life, like a garment that could not be removed. The senses recoil from suffering; faith blesses it as a gift from the hand of Jesus, a share in his cross which he deigns to let us carry with him.

And so the just who live by faith have their souls full of new ideas, new pleasures, new principles. New horizons open out in front of them, marvellous horizons illumined by a heavenly light whose beauty comes from the beauty of God. Absorbed in these new truths that the world has no notion of, believers have no choice but to start a new life. Anyone who sees this light and takes it at its true value holds it infinitely important, clings to it unshakeably, follows it in everything and refuses to be turned aside by anything.

La Dernière place, pp. 118-121

Because Charles was so acutely aware of having been saved, brought back to life by the mercy of God, an immense trust and an immense love sprang up in his heart. He based his trust on what Jesus said to the woman weeping at his feet in the house of Simon the Pharisee, "I tell you, her sins, her many sins, must have been forgiven her or she would not have shown such great love. It is the one who is forgiven little who shows little love." [Lk 7:47] Charles would cite this text again when he wrote to Fr. Huvelin to submit his first foundation projects to him [See letter to Fr. Huvelin, 22 September 1893]. And because his experience went so deep, he never forgot he was a pardoned sinner and that "*the Son of Man came to seek out and save what was lost*". [Lk 19:10]

> *We can hope. We are precisely the ones Jesus came to save, for we are being lost. Yes, without him we are perishing at every moment. We can hope, for whatever we may be guilty of, Jesus wants to save us. The more sinful we are, the closer to death, the deeper our state of despair for our body and our soul, the more it can be said that Jesus wants to save us, for he came to save what was about to be lost. We must never be discouraged but always hope. We are on the edge of a gulf, we are about to sink, we deserve to sink, we truly ought to sink because of our measureless ingratitude, we are sinking. We are just the ones Jesus came to save. He wants to save us because we are sinking. He is infinitely good and infinitely powerful. To the very last, as long as there is a breath of life left, all can hope in him.*
>
> *En vue de Dieu seul,* p. 272

He often repeated that it was those who were the least whom Jesus chose, not only to save them but also to make them his special friends:

> *"He saw Levi sitting by the customs house" [Mk 2:14] There is no state so contemptible, so worthy of contempt, where you cannot reach in and pull people out, not only to save them but to make them your favourites, to raise them to great holiness. You reach down into the dust of the road to recover lost coins that people have been trampling on, and make them shine like new. We must never lose hope, not for ourselves or for others or for anyone, no matter how sunk in vice. Someone may seem to have choked off the last shred of goodness inside, but we must never lose hope, not only that such a one may be saved but even may climb the heights of holiness. God is mighty enough to do it. The Good Shepherd can bring sheep back to his fold at the eleventh hour as at the first hour. His goodness, like his power, has no limits. To be always ready to hope is an obligation for us.*

> *En vue de Dieu seul,* p. 289

Later Brother Charles would find the words to communicate this strong hope in God's mercy with great understanding and kindness to people tormented by a sense of their wretchedness, as in this letter to his friend L. Massignon:

Peace and trust. Hope. Don't dwell on yourself.
Our moral wretchedness is a muddy swamp that
should often inspire us to humble ourselves, but
we shouldn't always have our eyes on it. We
should also turn our eyes to the Beloved, and
keep them much more often on him, on his beauty
and his infinite love with which he graciously
loves us. When you love you forget yourself and
think of the one you love. If we're constantly
thinking of how unworthy of being loved we are,
that's not love.

Œuvres Spirituelles de Charles de Jesus père
de Foucauld, p. 774

II

CAPTIVATED
BY JESUS OF NAZARETH

A Fascination with the Incarnation

It was probably in 1888 that Charles heard a phrase in one of Fr. Huvelin's sermons which, as he later said, was to *"engrave itself indelibly in my soul"*:

> *Jesus took the last place so utterly that no one has ever been able to get it away from him.*

It was about the same time, the end of the year 1888, that Fr. Huvelin urged him to go on pilgrimage to the Holy Land. Why? Perhaps because he sensed that this explorer was a man to whom places meant a lot. Before he would be able to understand his faith better with his mind, he would need to see and touch something. This is just what happened. When he was there in the places where the Incarnation actually came about, Brother Charles had a powerful insight into how real it was. It is a bit like what St. Thomas said: he needed to see with his own eyes and touch with his hands just how much God had loved us, just how much he had become one of us, poor among the poor.

Arriving in Palestine in December, he went first to Bethlehem to spend Christmas. There the tiny baby of the manger reached out to him from his weakness and poverty:

> *After spending Christmas 1888 at Bethlehem and hearing midnight Mass and receiving Holy Communion at the grotto, two or three days later I went back to Jerusalem. The sweetness I had felt praying in that grotto where the voices of Jesus, Mary and Joseph once echoed and where I was so close to them had been inexpressible. But it took only an hour's walk, and the church of the Holy Sepulchre, Calvary and the Mount of Olives loomed up ahead of me. Whether I wanted it or not, my thoughts had to change direction so I could be there at the foot of the Cross.*
> Letter to Fr. Jerome, 21 December 1896

A few days later at the beginning of January, he arrived at Nazareth. There he discovered, as he wrote to one of his cousins, *"the humble, obscure existence of the divine workman of Nazareth"*. [Letter to L. de Foucauld, 12 April 1897]

Going to Nazareth had a decisive impact. The shock echoed in his heart like a call. The vocation it awakened in

Places where Charles de Foucauld lived

him would express itself in an ever intensifying desire. Seven years later as he was leaving the Trappists, he wrote:

> *I am thirsting to lead at last the life I've been looking for these seven years and more. I glimpsed it, guessed at it, as I was walking the streets of Nazareth where the feet of Our Lord had trod, a poor craftsman lost in extreme lowliness and obscurity.*
>
> Letter to M. de Bondy, 24 June 1896

Charles' route had now been given a direction. Charles had been captured by the mystery of God's humility and throughout his life he would never stop contemplating it.

Meditating on the birth of Jesus, he wrote on 6 November 1897:

> *The Incarnation takes its source from God's goodness. But there is one thing about it so marvellous that it shines like a dazzling sign: the infinite humility such a mystery contains. God, the Infinite, the Almighty, becomes human, the least of all human beings. For myself, let me always seek the last place of all, so that I can be as lowly as my master. I must walk with him step by step as his faithful disciple and live with my God who lived his whole life in the last place and gave me such an example of this in his birth.*
>
> *La Derniere place,* p. 50 & 53

And he added directly afterwards:

> *"He went down with them and came to Nazareth and lived under their authority." You went down to live the life of poor working people, toiling for their living...at Nazareth.*
>
> *La Derniere place,* p. 54

To speak of "the last place" and "extreme lowliness" for Jesus' life at Nazareth may seem exaggerated. Charles was probably influenced by his times. Especially in the aristocratic classes he came from, manual work was quite looked down upon. Besides that, Nazareth, which was then under Turkish rule, would have seemed quite squalid to the eyes of a traveller from Paris.

But perhaps we should look deeper and remember that he had just been to Bethlehem, then to Jerusalem. What had such impact on him was to realise that Jesus had chosen to take on the conditions of the poor from his birth to his death. He would turn to this discovery for inspiration all through his life, as we see from this meditation written in June 1916, at Tamanrasset:

> *"He went down with them and came to Nazareth": all his life he did nothing but go down. He went down when he took flesh, he went down by becoming a little baby, he went down by obeying, he went down by becoming poor, abandoned, outcast, persecuted, tortured,*

taking always and everywhere the last place.
Voyageur dans la nuit, p. 208

The central insight of Brother Charles' faith is here. It is in profound harmony with the heart of Christian revelation. How can we keep from thinking of the Suffering Servant in Isaiah? The Apostles keep referring to this Servant in their early preaching. Paul too has this in mind in the Servant hymn in the letter to the Philippians.

The Way of Discipleship

Thus Charles' pilgrimage to the Holy Land can be summed up as a fascination with a person. It is not so much an event that can be marked on a calendar, but rather a call. The inner energies this call awoke would show themselves throughout Charles' life.

The God who had revealed himself to him in the figure of Jesus of Nazareth now drew Charles to leave everything and follow him:

> *The Gospel showed me that the first command-ment is to love God with all one's heart and that love had to be the beginning and the end of everything. Everybody knows that the first effect of love is imitation. So what I had to do next was to enter the Order where I could find the closest imitation of Jesus. I didn't feel I was made for*

A portrait of Brother Marie-Albéric in his Trappist habit
(painted posthumously from a photograph taken at Beni Abbès).

preaching like Jesus in his public life, so I needed to imitate him in his hidden life as a poor and humble workman at Nazareth. I thought nothing would offer me this way of life better than a Trappist monastery.

Letter to H. de Castries, 14 August 1901

Charles' motives are clear: because of Jesus and his Gospel, he wanted to take up the way of discipleship and let Jesus take possession of him and lead him on.

Why did I enter the Trappists? Out of love, pure love. I love our Lord Jesus Christ, though I wish my heart could love him better and more. Still, I love him and I cannot bear to lead a life different from his. I do not want a comfortable, respected life when his was the hardest and most reviled that ever was.

Letter to H. Duvreyier, 24 April 1890

Charles clearly felt that following in the footsteps of Jesus of Nazareth required him to become quite concretely poor the way his master had been:

My God, I do not know if some people can see you poor and willingly remain rich. Can they realise they are so much above their master, their Beloved, and not want to be like you in every way within their power, to be like you most of all in your lowliness? I'm sure they must love you, my

God, but I think there's something missing in their love. In any case, I for my part cannot conceive a love without a need, a compelling need, to be alike, to do the same, and most of all to share all the hardships and trials and troubles of life. To be rich and secure and live comfortably off my property, when you were poor and needy and toiled for your living. As for me, I couldn't do it, my God. I couldn't love like that. The servant should not be greater than his master.

La Dernière place, p. 175

On 15 January 1890, he said good-bye to his family, parting from his cousin Marie with his heart breaking. He arrived at the Trappist Monastery of Our Lady of the Snows on 16 January.

A few months later, he was sent to another monastery, recently founded at Akbes in Syria (under Turkish rule). The buildings were makeshift and life was harder there. Brother Marie Alberic (his religious name as a Trappist) was happy.

But nostalgia for Nazareth was not slow in coming back. Soon he was writing to Fr. Huvelin:

You hope I've poverty enough. No, we are poor in comparison with the rich, but we are not as poor as our Lord was, not poor the way I was in Morocco, not poor like St. Francis.

Letter to Fr. Huvelin, 5 November 1890

One day he was sent to keep vigil at the bedside of a poor Catholic who was dying in a small village nearby, and he reflected:

> *What a difference between this house and where I live. I pine for Nazareth.*
>> Letter to M. de Bondy, 10 April 1894

A desire began to grow in his heart then. Since there was no order that offered the poverty and the form of life he was dreaming of, why not found a little religious congregation which would have no other aim but to live a life like Jesus at Nazareth?

He brought it up to Fr. Huvelin in 1893:

> *Wouldn't it be possible to form a little congregation to lead this life? We would live only from the work of our own hands, like our Lord, who did not take up collections or live from offerings, nor did he have foreign labourers working for him while he sat back and supervised. Couldn't a few people be found to follow our Lord like this, to follow him by following all his counsels? They would renounce all ownership of property, whether collective or individual, and consequently they could absolutely forbid themselves what our Lord prohibited: all lawsuits, accusations, and defence of their rights. They would make it an absolute duty to give alms: if they have two habits they must give one of them away: if they*

have something to eat they must give some to those who have nothing, and not keep anything for the next day. They would follow all the examples of Jesus' hidden life and all the counsels that came from his lips.

It would be a life of work and prayer, not with two categories of religious as the Trappists have, but only one, as St. Benedict wanted it to be. There would just be long silent prayer, the rosary, the holy Mass. Our liturgy closes the door on Arabs, Turks, Armenians and such, who are good Catholics but do not know a word of our languages. I would so like to see little nests like these set up, and in them a fervent and hard-working life, reproducing the life of our Lord, under his keeping and with the protection of Mary and Joseph. There should be one near every mission in the East, where life is so isolated. It would offer a refuge to the souls of the people in these countries whom God calls to serve him and to love him single-heartedly.

Is this a dream, dear Father? Is it an illusion from the devil or is it an idea and an invitation that comes from God? If I could be sure it came from God, I would start on it today and not tomorrow and do what I need to do to take up this path. When I think about the concept, I find it ideal. But when I think about the one who conceived it, and conceived it so ardently, I do not think I see in him the stuff God usual-

ly uses to do good things. It is true that if I made a start, then if the project came from God he would be the one to give the increase. Something else gives me courage to undertake a project so little suited to a sinner of my unworthiness: the Lord said that the one who had sinned greatly would be the one who should love greatly.

Letter to Fr. Huvelin, 22 September 1893

He had spelled his project out clearly. And yet Brother Marie Alberic did not leave the Trappists until January 1897. Why did he wait so long?

This was a man of impulsive, impatient nature, who wanted to put the ideas he conceived into action immediately. But there was a single desire taking hold of him more and more: to let himself be led by the Will of God. And so, for this decisive step he would wait for God's Will to be confirmed for him by Fr. Huvelin and by his Trappist superiors. He trusted that he would find his path through them.

Perhaps he also vaguely guessed that he had first to surrender this project so dear to him to God, to make a sacrifice of it, one might say.

The meditation he wrote just at this time on the sacrifice of Abraham may reveal what was going on in his own heart:

Saint Abraham, blessed are you. Saint Isaac, who let yourself be tied to the altar without resistance, blessed are you. My God, who plant such virtues in human beings, blessed are you for all ages without end.

Love means obeying you, obeying you with just such promptness and such faith, though our heart is breaking and our mind in turmoil, though every idea we have held be turned upside down. Love means unrestricted, unhesitating sacrifice of what we hold most dear, to your Will. The sacrifice of the only son, of what our heart wants most. Love means trading all our desires for nothing but suffering, out of love for the Lord.

This is what you did, St. Abraham. This is what you were to do, O Son of God, when you came down from heaven to earth to live the life you lived and die the death you died.

My Lord and my God, make me do the same and follow your Holy Will. Saint Abraham and Saint Isaac, pray for me.

Written at Rome, November 1896.
Qui peut resistir à Dieu, pp. 64-5

In 1896, Fr. Huvelin agreed to Brother Marie Alberic's plan. The date when he would have to either make his final vows or leave the order was coming up. His superiors would have to make a decision about him.

At this crucial moment at the end of 1896, he was feeling a remarkable self-surrender. He asked for nothing and just trusted God to take care of everything. We know this from a letter he wrote to Brother Jerome, a young Trappist he had met at the monastery of Staouëli and to whom he had been asked to be like an older brother. He wrote to him first about obedience:

Obedience is the last, the highest and most perfect of the degrees of love. Here you cease to exist in yourself, you become nothing, you die as Jesus did on the Cross.

Letter to Fr. Jerome, 24 January 1897

And a little further on he wrote:

I've had to practise obedience a lot just this week, and obedience is still what I have to practise, along with courage.

For the last three and a half years I've been asking to pass from the status of choir monk to that of lay brother, either in the Order or in another religious order with houses in the East. I think this is my vocation: to go down.

With the permission of my confessor, I had submitted this request. My superiors ordered me, before they would grant it, to go and spend some time at Staouëli. When I got there, to my great surprise I was told to go to Rome. And here I thought I would have to wait a long time still before I was given the permission I longed for. But our good Father General has called me in, examined my motives, reflected on my vocation, called together his Council, and they all unanimously agree that the Will of God is for me to follow this path of lowliness, poverty and humble manual labour, life as a workman of Nazareth that the Workman of Nazareth himself has been inspiring in me for so long. I got the news yesterday from our dear, wonderful Father General, whose kindness touches me so much.

But the point where I had need of obedience was before his decision. I had promised God that I would do everything Reverend Father told me after the examination of my vocation he was about to undertake and everything my confessor told me to do. So if they had said to me, "You will make your solemn vows in ten days" and later on "You will be ordained a priest," I would have obeyed with joy, sure that I was doing the will of God. For I was seeking absolutely nothing but the will of God, and I had superiors who were seeking only his will too. So it was impossible that God would not make his will known.

From the same letter

On 23 January 1897, he was thus given permission to leave the Trappist Order.

On 14 February he made private vows in the presence of his confessor, a vow of perpetual chastity and a vow *"never to have in his possession or at his disposal more than a poor workman would have."*

And on 17 February, he set sail for the Holy Land. A few days later Fr. Huvelin wrote to him:

Yes, like you my dear child, I picture you in the East. I prefer Capernaum or Nazareth or some Franciscan convent, not in the convent, but in its shadow. Just ask to use the spiritual resources of the convent and live in poverty at the door. This, my dear friend, is what I can see possible.
Don't think about gathering followers around you and still less of giving them a rule. Live your life, and if followers come, live the same life together. But make no rules. On this I insist.
Letter from Fr. Huvelin, 27 January 1897

III

FROM NAZARETH TO BENI ABBÈS

Hermit at Nazareth

It was the Poor Clares of Nazareth who let Charles stay and accepted to take him on as a hired man. He lived in a tool shed and christened it *"Hermitage of our Lady of Perpetual Help."*

The life he led was still deeply marked by his recent experience in the monastery. He had more time at this period of his life than at any other for reading, praying and meditating silently in the shelter of the cloister.

You ask me for details about my life. I am staying in a solitary shed. It's inside the Sisters' enclosure and I am their happy servant. I am alone there. It is a gem of a hermitage, perfectly solitary. I get up when my Guardian Angel wakes me and I pray and meditate till time for the Angelus. Then I go over to the Franciscan convent and go down to the grotto that was part of the Holy Family's house. I stay there till about 6:00 in the morning, saying my rosary and hearing

Masses. It delights me deeply to look at the rock walls that Jesus once had before his eyes and touched with his hands. At 6:00 I go back to the Sisters, set up for their Mass and serve it at 7:00. Then I do whatever I am told to. If there's an errand I do it, but that's very rare. In general I spend my day doing odd jobs in my little room near the sacristy. I stay in the chapel from 5:00 to 7:30 in the evening. After that I go back to my dear hermitage. I read till 9:00 and go to bed. I read during the meals; I eat alone. I see nobody at all but my confessor once a week to go to confession and the Sisters when they have to tell me something, which happens rarely.

Letter to R. de Blic, 25 November 1897

Almost all Brother Charles' meditations on the Scriptures come from these years at Nazareth. It was truly "at the table of the Word as at the table of the Eucharist" that he fed his prayer and his desire to be like Jesus. His desire burned higher and higher.

We must try to let Jesus' spirit fill us by reading his words and examples over and over, meditating on them over and over. They should do in our souls what the drop of water does when it falls again and again on the paving stone, always at the same place.

Œuvres Spirituelles, p. 144

Receive the Gospel. It is by the Gospel, according to the Gospel, that we will be judged. It is not by the book of some spiritual guide or some learned scholar or some saint but by the Gospel of Jesus, the words of Jesus, the examples of Jesus, the counsels of Jesus, the teachings of Jesus.
L'imitation du Bien-aimé, p. 204

The Eucharist meant to Charles that Jesus was there very close, very really present.

Jesus, my Lord, you are in the Holy Eucharist. You are here, a metre away from me, in this tabernacle. How close by you are, my God, my Saviour, my Jesus, my Brother.
La Derniere place, p. 81

He wanted this presence to take possession of him:

My God, grant me a continual awareness of your presence. And grant me that awed love that we feel in the presence of the one we love passionately and that makes us stay by the beloved person without being able to take our eyes away.
La Derniere place, p. 41

In fact, his adoration was often a matter of staying there in faith while his prayer was arid and unrewarding:

When I'm in front of the Blessed Sacrament I

63

have a hard time staying there to pray for very long. I'm in a strange state. Everything seems empty and hollow to me, worthless and without point, except for staying at Our Lord's feet and looking at him. And then when I go to his feet, I'm dry as a bone, without a word or a thought in my head, and often, sad to say, I end up going to sleep. I reason myself into reading, but the whole thing seems empty to me.

Letter to Fr. Huvelin, 22 October 1898

The depth of his faith saved him from the risks of an individualistic piety. The Eucharist for him meant Jesus offering his life in intercession for all people, and to love Jesus meant participation in Jesus' self-giving love.

Ever fascinated by the mystery of the Incarnation, he meditated on its implications for the believer: the requirement to love one another.

See in the Incarnation love for all people, the love God has for them. Therefore you must love them after his example, to be perfect just as your heavenly Father is perfect. This love is active and alive. It is deep. It made God cover at a single leap the distance that separates the finite from the infinite. It made him choose an unprecedented means for our salvation, the Incarnation. God himself came to live on the earth.

Crier l'Evangile, pp. 18-19

When he meditated on the Visitation during the same retreat, he caught a glimpse of the apostolic dimension of the life of Nazareth:

> *I had hardly taken flesh when I asked my Mother to carry me to the house where John was to be born. Before I was even born myself, I was at work on the sanctification of the human race, and I prompted my Mother to work with me.*
>
> *And to all the other people to whom I give myself I say: Work with me as my Mother did, without words, in silence, in the midst of people who do not know me. Carry me among them by setting up an altar there, a tabernacle. Take the Gospel there not by preaching it with your lips, but preaching it with your example, not by proclaiming it but by living it.*
>
> *Crier l'Evangile*, pp. 21-22

> *Our whole existence, our whole being, should cry the Gospel from the rooftops. Our whole personality should spell Jesus; all our acts, all our life should proclaim that we belong to Jesus and show a mirror of Gospel life.*
>
> *La Bonté de Dieu*, p. 285

His years at Nazareth were thus a time of desert for Brother Charles, when "God spoke to his heart" and when his desire grew deeper:

"The Visitation", drawn by Brother Charles.

What I'm secretly dreaming of, without admitting it to myself, what I can't help dreaming of, is something very simple, for just a few people. It would be like those communities in the early Church. A few people gathered together to lead the life of Nazareth, to live by their work the way the Holy Family did, and practise the Nazareth virtues as they contemplate Jesus.

Letter to Fr. Huvelin, 22 October 1898

But the desert was also the place of trial and temptation. And Brother Charles often cast about as he looked for his path in those three years. We see that from his letters to Fr. Huvelin.

For several months he wondered if he ought to go back to the Trappists:

Sometimes I tell myself I could have done some good if I had stayed with the Trappists, that I would have been superior in two years, and with God's help I could have done some good in that little monastery at Akbes.

Letter to Fr. Huvelin, 16 January 1898

The abbess of the Poor Clares in Jerusalem, who had discovered who their hired man was, already pictured him chaplain of the convent and tried to convince him to become a priest, all the while encouraging him to plan his foundation.

There was a moment when, seeing the distress of a

poor widow, he thought of "selling himself" as a nurse with the Sisters of Charity to pay the widow's keep.

About that same time he heard of some property for sale at the top of the Mount of the Beatitudes. The idea infatuated him and made him dream of founding a group of priest-hermits there.

The result of my Holy Week was that I decided to leave St. Clare's convent. I'm "as pampered as a prize pup" here, if you'll excuse the expression. I wanted to set myself up as a hermit in a vacant spot somewhere in the hills over-looking Nazareth and bear the cross of Jesus there in a life of poverty and work. I had never thought a moment about the Mount of the Beatitutdes nor about becoming a priest. But suddenly here I am with the three things at once, fitting together and presenting themselves to me almost under the form of a logical conclusion.
Letter to Fr. Huvelin, 26 April 1900

The more I think about it, the more I find it a necessity to be ordained "for the service of holy poverty"—that is, ordained as a hermit. This means being ordained by a bishop who would give tentative approval to a rule I've been following for a year and a half and that I've been thinking about for a long, long, time. This spring it will be seven years since I wrote you from Akbes with the outlines of my project: to lead the

*life of Our Lady in the mystery of her Visitation,
along with a few companions. That is, to sanctify
the unbelievers of mission countries. Silently,
without preaching, we would bring Jesus in the
Blessed Sacrament and the practice of the evangelical virtues into their midst.*

Letter to Fr. Huvelin, 7 May 1900

Fr. Huvelin was getting tired of all these projects and
was far from enthusiastic: *"Your projects frighten me.
I do not think that this idea of priest-hermits comes
from God. Still, if you feel irresistibly drawn to it, take
your rule, go to the Patriarch of Jerusalem, throw yourself at his feet and ask him for light. For my part, my
child, I am in the dark. I see nothing but objections, and
I fear a spirit of self-seeking underneath your devotion
and your piety."* [Letter from Fr. Huvelin to Brother
Charles, 20 May 1900]

Brother Charles got no understanding from the
Patriarch, and so he gave up all his projects and
returned peacefully to Nazareth.

And then Fr. Huvelin perceived that through all
this casting about for the path something had become
ripe, and he wrote: *"Now I think that it may work. I
think you will go towards the Lord and will lead others
there and are learning to live the Gospel. I know the
Master was guiding it all. It was not that you had to
make an idea succeed, it was the will of God you had
to find. You had to leave it to grow of itself, gently,
peacefully, in littleness and utter lowliness, like Jesus*

at his beginnings in Bethlehem and during the long incubation at Nazareth." [Letter from Fr. Huvelin to Brother Charles, 25 July 1900]

Take the Banquet to the Poor

On 16 August 1900, Brother Charles went back to France to prepare himself for the priesthood. He spent several months at Our Lady of the Snows.

Before his ordination he made a "retreat of election" [See *Seul avec Dieu*, p. 77ff] He centred it on three of Jesus' sayings that were specially dear to him:

> *"Into your hands I commit my spirit."*
> *"He came to bring fire to the earth."*
> *"He came to seek out and save what was lost."*

And his future began to clear. He would not go back to Nazareth:

> *It is not where the ground is most hallowed that I must go, but where the souls are in the greatest need.*
>
> *Seul avec Dieu,* p. 83

> *My retreats before being ordained to the diaconate and to the priesthood showed me that I ought to lead the life of Nazareth, which is my vocation, not in the Holy Land I love so well but among*

the people whose souls were most sick, the sheep who were most forsaken. I am the minister of a divine banquet which should be offered not to our brothers, relatives and rich neighbours, but to the crippled and the blind, to the most forsaken souls, where priests are most in shortage.

When I was young I had travelled through Algeria and Morocco. Morocco, as big as France and with a population of ten million people, did not have a single priest away from the coastal areas. In the Algerian Sahara, 7 or 8 times as big as France and more densely populated than used to be thought, there were a dozen missionaries. No people seemed to me more forsaken than these. And so I sought and obtained permission from the Apostolic Prefect of the Sahara to settle in the Algerian Sahara.

Letter to Bishop Caron, 8 April 1905

On 9 June 1901, Charles was ordained a priest. On the 23rd he was already writing to his friend H. de Castries, who knew the Sahara well, to ask his advice about where to settle. He explained what he wanted:

To start a house on the Moroccan border, not a Trappist monastery, not a big and wealthy convent or a farming enterprise, but a sort of humble little hermitage where several poor monks could live from a few fruit trees and a little barley they harvest themselves. They would live strictly cloistered, in penitence and adoration of the Blessed Sacrament, and not go out of their enclosure or preach but offer hospitality to all who come, good or bad, friend or foe, Muslim or Christian.

This would be evangelisation not by the word but by the presence of the Blessed Sacrament, the offering of the holy sacrifice, prayer, penitence, the practice of the evangelical virtues, and charity, a brotherly charity offered to all. We would share our bread to the last mouthful with the poor, with our guests, with strangers, and receive any person as our beloved brother or sister.

Letter to H. de Castries, 23 June 1901

The Word of God taken seriously is dangerous.

On the threshold of this new step, Brother Charles felt within him the fire that burned the prophet Jeremiah, the fire Jesus came to bring on earth. Like Elijah after the vision on Horeb, God had sent him back to the streets of the world, where people struggle, where Jesus continues to suffer and die, where the poor and the outcast are waiting for the good news.

Charles did not suspect that in letting himself be thus guided by the logic of the Incarnation he was blazing new trails for the way of contemplation. What inspired him to go back to what he had left was the love of his beloved Jesus, the desire to be with him and walk with him where he had met him, "*on the streets of Nazareth,*" as a poor, obscure man in the crowd.

His time at Nazareth had been marked by long contemplation of the Eucharist. Now this would blossom into a Eucharistic life, in which Brother Charles discovered more and more that communion in the Body and Blood of Christ destined him to become, like Christ, a man devoured.

He rediscovered what Saint John Chrysostom had long ago affirmed: *"The sacrament of the altar is not to be separated from the sacrament of the neighbour."*

God's startling choice of the dispossessed showed Brother Charles what he hadn't seen before. It led him now into a life just as contemplative, but one that was mingled with others and more and more under the sign of hospitality, service, and brotherly sharing with the poorest.

It was at Beni Abbès, the Algerian oasis closest to the Moroccan border, that Brother Charles would build his hermitage:

> *Not far from the fort and the oasis, yet in a solitary place, I've found a little hollow which is arid but irrigable (water is abundant at Beni Abbès). With the help of God I'm going to make it into a garden, and on the flank of the hill men from the garrison and the Arab Bureau have started building me a dwelling. I am deeply grateful for their kindness and charity. They are using mud bricks and palm trunks and making a chapel, three cells and a guest room. I will move in tomorrow. That's how fast they've been working.*

Letter to H. de Castries, 29 November 1901

"Whatever You Do to the Least of These"

Charles drew up a very precise set of rules for himself as a monk. He even marked off his enclosure with a line of small stones. He decreed he would cross the line only in case of necessity, but he never built a wall and he kept his door constantly open.

> *I want all the people here, be they Christians, Muslims, Jews or whatever, to see me as their brother, a universal brother. They have started calling my house "the fraternity" and that gives me pleasure.*
>
> Letter to M. de Bondy, 7 January 1902

Receiving guests would quickly disrupt his way of life:

> *Guests, poor people, slaves, visitors – they don't leave me a minute's peace. I'm the only one, with all the work of the monastery to do. I finished the little guest house on the 15th and since then every day we've had guests to lodge and to feed morning and evening. The place hasn't been empty once. There are as many as eleven a night, not counting an old cripple who lives there permanently. I have 60 to 100 visitors a day, quite often if not always.*
>
> Letter to Dom Martin, 7 February 1902

It's the same thing every day, poor people, sick people, one after the other. I reproach myself interiorly for not spending enough time in prayer and purely spiritual things. By day people never stop knocking at my door, and at night when it would be a good time for it I fall asleep like a wretch. It shames me and saddens me that sleep takes up more room than I want it to. I haven't time for it and it takes its own.

Letter to Fr. Huvelin, 15 December 1902

Attentive to whatever people might need, he let soldiers posted at Beni Abbès come for prayer and the sacraments. They had no other spiritual assistance.

The willingness of the soldiers around me, and a piety I never hoped to find in them, allow me to hold benediction of the Blessed Sacrament every evening without exception. I precede it with a reading from the Holy Gospel and a short explanation: I can't get over it that they want to listen to me. After benediction I lead a short prayer.

Letter to M. de Bondy, 30 December 1901

With surprise I'm seeing myself pass from the contemplative life to a life of ministry. I've been led to it in spite of myself by people's needs.

Letter to M. de Blic, 17 January 1902

Brother Charles welcomes visitors to Beni Abbès.

But the ones who were farthest away were the ones he wanted to be close to:

Occupy myself specially with the lost sheep, the sinners, the wicked. Mustn't leave the 99 sheep who have gone astray to stay serenely in the fold with the one faithful sheep. Conquer the natural severity I feel towards sinners and replace it with compassion, interest, zeal, diligent care.
Seul avec Dieu, p. 100

He bought freedom for some slaves and baptised a four-year-old child and an old woman, and started dreaming about the birth of a little Christian community.

Pray for my four children in Beni Abbès: Abd-Jesu, who has stayed with me and is becoming more and more of a dear, Paul, Pierre, and Marie. These are the feeble little beginnings of Christianity in these parts.
Letter to M. de Bondy, 21 January 1903

But he was aware how uncertain the enterprise was, and knew he had to leave things up to God:

Our little beginnings of Christianity here at Beni Abbès seem to be going back down to zero. May the will of Jesus be done. Paul left me in a rather painful way, and Pierre, whose parents live ten days' walk or so from here, wants to go back to them. Marie is going to have her cataracts operated on and if it works she won't have any more reason to stay and can go back to living on her own. There'll be only Abd-Jesu left. He's becoming more of a dear every day and I'm eager to see him in better hands than mine, with the Sisters of St. Vincent de Paul.

Letter to M. de Bondy, 2 March 1903

He took these tasks on because he was the only priest for hundreds of kilometres. But he didn't want it to lead him to any other kind of life than the imitation of Jesus at Nazareth, which was his chosen vocation. He wrote after a visit from his bishop:

Bishop Guérin seems to have a little, discrete tendency to push me gently towards transforming my life as a silent and hidden monk, my life of Nazareth, into life as a missionary. This tendency I shall not follow, for I believe I would be very unfaithful to God, who gave me a vocation to the hidden and silent life and not to the life of a man of words. Both monks and missionaries are apostles, but in different ways. On this point I shall not yield, and I'll keep following the path that I've lived well or poorly for 14 years, most often poorly, sad to say, but faithfully. I'll live Jesus' hidden life with others if Jesus sends them, alone if he leaves me alone.

Letter to Fr. Huvelin, 10 June 1903

By receiving the poorest, he discovered the conditions they lived in, and he was not slow to realise concretely how extremely oppressed they were.

> *I had believed and I had heard that slavery among the Muslims was a rather lenient affair. Now that I speak to many slaves a day on familiar terms, and particularly when I speak to them out of hearing of their masters, I can see how wrong I was. They are overworked (getting water for the palm plantations), beaten daily, underfed and underclothed, and if they try to run away – which happens frequently – there is an armed pursuit.*
>
> Letter to H. de Castries, 15 January 1902

Charles was a product of his times and did not call colonialism as such into question. But every time he witnessed flagrant injustices he took a forceful stand against them.

In front of the *"abomination of slavery"* he tried to do what he could. His door was open to the hungry and besides this he managed to redeem a few young slaves and gave them back their freedom. When he realised that the situation was being maintained with the complicity of the French authorities, he looked for a way to rouse public opinion. Throughout the year 1902, he wrote letter after letter.

To Dom Martin, the Abbot of Our Lady of the Snows, he expressed his indignation:

What you say is what I am doing concerning the slaves. But having said it, and giving them all the relief I can, I do not think my duty is over. I have to say, or get the appropriate people to say, "This is not allowed. Woe to you hypocrites," who print on your stamps and all around, Liberty, Equality, Fraternity, Human Rights, while you fasten slaves in irons. You throw into the dungeon those who counterfeit your banknotes while you allow children to be stolen from their parents and publicly sold. You punish the theft of a chicken while you permit the theft of a man. (In fact, almost all the slaves of this region were born free and kidnapped from their parents as children.)

Next, we must love our neighbour as ourselves and treat these poor people as we would like to be treated. We must keep any of those God has entrusted to us from being lost, and he entrusts to us all the people in our territory.

It's not for us to get involved in worldly government, no one is more convinced of that than I am. But we must love justice and hate evil, and when the worldly government commits a deep injustice towards those who are in some way under our care (I am the only priest in this prefecture for 300 km in any direction), we must tell them so. For we are the ones who on earth represent justice and truth, and we do not have the right to be "sleeping sentinels" and "dumb watchdogs" and "useless shepherds." [Is. 56:9-11, see Ez 34]

*In a word, I'm wondering if (presuming we com-
pletely agree about what should be done towards
the slaves) we mustn't speak out directly or indi-
rectly to make this injustice known in France.
Slavery is a sanctioned theft going on in our
regions, and we must say or get someone to say,
"Look what is happening. This is not allowed."
I have notified the Apostolic Prefect, maybe
that's enough. Far be it from me to want to
speak and write, but I do not want to betray my
children or fail to do for Jesus, living in his
members, what he needs. It is Jesus caught in
this wretched situation: "Whatever you did to
the least of these, you did to me." I don't want
to be a bad shepherd or a dumb watchdog. I'm
afraid I might sacrifice Jesus for my peace and
the quiet I'm so fond of, or for my cowardice
and natural timidity.*

Letter to Dom Martin, 7 February, 1902

He set out the problem in detail for his bishop and begged
him to intervene. He asked his advice on what to do:

*The biggest question is slavery. One of my friends
offered me a chance to put the matter into the
hands of Baron Cochin, a fervent anti-slavery
campaigner in the Chamber of Deputies. I did
not accept for the moment, as I wanted to leave
it up to you. But might you not be able to see M.
Cochin when you go to France soon?*

81

Going into long detail on the mistreatment inflicted on the slaves in the Saoura region and its oases seems the wrong approach to me. True, they are mistreated, but whether they are treated better or worse, the great injustice is that they are slaves!

Slavery is all the more unjust here. (It is always unjust for we are all children of Adam and commanded to "treat others as you would like them to treat you.") But besides the huge and monstrous injustice that is always at the root of slavery, there is a special injustice here: very few of the slaves are children of slaves. Almost all of them were kidnapped as children, either from the Sudan or from Touat, when they were 5 years old, or 10 or 15.

My beloved Father, I think the words of Jesus are an obligation on me: "Treat others as you would like them to treat you." I must do what I can for these poor people who are my children and who are yours even more so.

Letter to Bishop Guérin, 28 June 1902

Bishop Guérin was clearly horrified by Brother Charles' proposals and explained to him they were out of place. *"As for the slavery question, my very dear father, what can I say to you? More than on any other point I feel myself led to tell you: beware of your own zeal. Be very prudent, lay the sorrow you feel at the feet of Jesus. Beware of getting carried away by your zeal into active intervention. Slavery, there is no doubting it, is a social evil we cannot deplore enough, and Jesus' charity can never fill us too much. But to fight slavery, we must take into account the circumstances of the people we live among. We don't want to lose what means we may have for doing a little good by firing off bombshells which will bring no results besides. This is Archbishop Livinhac's private opinion. A public denunciation at present of what is going on in the South would only make it that much harder to do what we're now doing for people."*

Letter from Bishop Guérin to Brother Charles, 17 September 1902

Brother Charles submitted, but not without saying that the reasons given hadn't convinced him:

I will obey to the letter the line of conduct you've given me. The reasons you have been good enough to express to me with such affection and which have weight in that they come from you and from Archbishop Livinhac, do not leave me without regrets. Let me say it one last time, since a child-like soul should have no secrets from its Father and let everything come out without holding anything back inside, I regret that the representatives of Jesus content themselves with defending this cause "in whispers" (and not "from the rooftops"), for it is the cause of justice and charity.

Letter to Bishop Guérin, 30 September 1902

To Dom Martin he had written:

Where I fail to agree with you is that I find you much too easily accept evil and try to make the best of it.
Letter to Dom Martin, 17 March 1902

What Brother Charles was feeling strongly was that in such situations charity does not consist only of relieving suffering. When oppressive structures are intrinsically evil, you must go to the root of the evil and get rid of them.

The current regime must end and slavery must be abolished. Justice and right require it.
Letter to H. de Castries, 15 January 1902

No human power has the right to keep these wretched people in irons whom God created as free as we are. And if we allow their so-called masters to hold onto them by force and pursue them when they try to escape, if we give them back to their masters when they ask the French authorities for asylum, having hoped in vain to find protection and justice there, then we are robbing them of their most undeniable rights.
Letter to H. de Castries, 13 April 1902

The motivation at work when Brother Charles reacted against injustice was always the Word of God, the Gospel taken literally. He discovered increasingly the concrete solidarity with the poorest that Jesus' words commit us to: *"What you did to one of the least of these brothers or sisters of mine, you did to me":*

> *"I was hungry, I was thirsty, I was a stranger, I was naked, sick, in prison, and you never helped, welcomed, visited me. Whatever you did not do to the least of these, you did not do it to me." (Mt 25: 42-45)*
>
> *What a weighty saying. It is not there for us to make up commentaries about but to believe. We must see clearly that what we could have done for someone and did not do, it is Our Lord we have neglected to do it for.*
>
> *He did not say all the good we refused to do, no, all the good we did not do, all we could have done and neglected to do. The passerby who is poor, naked, a stranger, in trouble, asks nothing from us, but that person is a member of Jesus, a part of Jesus, a portion of Jesus. We let the person go by us and give him none of what he needs: it is Jesus we have let go by.*
>
> *This emphatically means we owe ourselves to our neighbours, body and soul. We owe our neighbours our hearts and our minds. This is what the example of Our Lord should say to us when he sums up his life in a single sentence: "The Son of Man came to serve and to give his life as a ransom for many."*
>
> *Aux Plus Petits de mes Frères,* p. 92-3

Brother Charles during his time at Beni Abbès.

A few months before his death, Brother Charles was to write to his friend Louis Massignon:

I think there is no saying in the Gospel that made a deeper impression on me and more transformed my life than this one: "Whatever you did to one of the least of these you did it to me."

If we remember that these are the words of Uncreated Truth and come from the same lips that said, "This is my Body, this is my Blood," how compellingly we are moved to seek out Jesus and love him in the "least ones," the sinners, the poor.

Letter to Louis Massignon, 1 August 1916

Brother Charles' conviction that Jesus is just as really present in any person suffering poverty and oppression as he is in the Eucharist was not only to transform his life but to unify it as well. It is the same love that made him spend hours before the Blessed Sacrament which incited him to commit himself to the liberation of the slaves in whom Jesus was suffering and dying.

IV

A BROTHER'S PRESENCE AT THE HEART OF THE DESERT

The Call of the Hoggar: Move on Again?

When he had chosen Beni Abbès, Brother Charles had gone as far away as he could go. But now a way into the South was opening up, a road into Tuareg country, to the Hoggar.

His friend Laperrine wrote to him at length about it in June 1903. Among other things, he told Charles about the remarkable actions of a Tuareg woman during a battle between some Tuaregs and some French soldiers. Her name was Tarichat Oult Ibdakane. *"She stood up against letting the tribesmen finish off the wounded and took them home and cared for them. When Attisi came back wounded from the fight and wanted to finish off the wounded prisoners himself, she wouldn't let him into her house. When the soldiers were well, she got them back to Tripoli."* [Letter from H. Laperrine, June 1903]

Brother Charles found this admirable and straight away composed in his journal a letter he wanted his bishop to write to this woman:

The first commandment of religion is to love God with all our heart. The second is to love all people without exception, as we love ourselves. With admiration and thanksgiving to God to see how well you practise love towards your fellow human beings, we write you this letter. We want you to know that among Christians, all the religious people who will hear about you will bless you and praise God for your virtues. They will ask God to grant you all blessings in this world and give you glory in heaven. We are also writing to ask you earnestly to pray for us, for we are convinced that God, who has put into your heart a will to love him and serve him, will hear the prayers you send up to him.

R. Bazin, *Charles de Foucauld*, p. 268

From then on Brother Charles began to feel a call to go to the Hoggar. He knew that he could join a military convoy to that region that his friend Laperrine was organizing. He began debating and struggling with himself about it.

My nature recoils from it exceedingly. I shudder – and am ashamed of it – at the thought of leaving Beni Abbès, where it is so calm at the foot of the altar, and throwing myself into travelling. I dread travelling enormously now. My reason too comes up with drawbacks to the idea. Am I to leave the tabernacle at Beni Abbès empty, go

Algeria and the Sahara.

away from this place where there just might be fighting (though not very likely), and waste my energies in these travels, which are no good for the soul? Would I not glorify God more by adoring him in solitude? Aren't solitude and the life of Nazareth my vocation?

After reason has said all that, I see before me those vast regions without a priest. I see myself the only priest able to go there, and more and more intensely I feel an urge to go. I'd like to go at least once. According to how it turns out, according to what the experience shows me, I'll decide whether to go back again or not. In spite of what my reason tells me and my nature's dread of being away from here, more and more I feel inside myself a strong urge to make this trip.

Letter to Fr. Huvelin, 13 December 1903

Thus it is by his deepest inner feelings, where his desires most match the desires of Jesus, that Brother Charles discerns the will of God. The sign is his inward urge, stronger than all the arguments of his reason.

His single-minded passion is still the same one: to let Jesus lead him, fill him and transform him by his words and examples. We can feel that Charles is becoming freer and more malleable in God's hands.

There's just one item of good I see in myself: it's my constant will to do what pleases God most, always and in everything. But as for carrying it

out, what a lot of falls.
Letter to Fr. Huvelin, 17 September 1907

His bishop was initially very hesitant about the plan but finally gave permission. After four months of exhausting treks through the desert, Brother Charles arrived in the Hoggar in May of 1904. He was immediately captivated by the place.

He wrote to Fr. Huvelin:

> *I'm living from one day to the next. As long as I can usefully stay in this country and others haven't come to replace me, I shall stay here. There needs to be somebody at a post like this.*
> *At the moment I'm a tent-dwelling nomad, changing places constantly. It's a good thing for the beginnings, for it lets me meet a lot of people and see a lot of regions, but as soon as I can settle down and stay somewhere permanently, I shall.*
> Letter to Fr. Huvelin, 15 July 1904

He had thus taken a new step. His attitude towards it came more than ever from his insights into Jesus of Nazareth. He did not seek out a solitary place to build his hermitage, but one accessible to everybody:

> *It is love which must focus your life of prayer, not distance from my children. See me in them. And as I did at Nazareth, live beside them, rapt in God.*
> *Carnet de Beni Abbés*, p. 110

When he looked back on what he had been doing up till then, it made him want an approach that was humbler and more unobtrusive than at Beni Abbès:

> *Lead the life of Jesus at Nazareth by the rule of the Little Brothers of the Sacred Heart. Be as little and as poor as Jesus was at Nazareth. Not try, as I did at Beni Abbès, to get a nest ready for my companions. God will give the nest if he sends the souls. Not try, as I did at Beni Abbès, to give away a lot in alms. If I have anything over, just give that. That was how Jesus, Mary and Joseph did it at Nazareth. Not try on my own to provide alms and hospitality as a fraternity of 25 Little Brothers would be able to do it. When in doubt, always do as Jesus did at Nazareth.*
>
> *Carnet de Beni Abbès*, p. 102

The following year he was back on the trails of the Hoggar:

> *In everything and for everything, take the life of Nazareth as my object, whether alone or with a few brothers, until such time as it becomes really possible to lead a life completely as Little Brothers and Little Sisters in a cloistered Nazareth. Let Nazareth be my model, in all its simplicity and breadth, using my rule as a handbook of guidelines which will sometimes help me find the way to the life of Nazareth.*
>
> *For example, until the Little Brothers and Little*

Sisters are duly established, no habit, like Jesus at Nazareth. No cloister, like Jesus at Nazareth. No withdrawn, out-of-the-way habitations, but a house near a village, like Jesus at Nazareth. No less than 8 hours of work a day (manual or other sorts, but manual as much as possible), like Jesus at Nazareth.

Carnet de Tamanraset, p. 46

And in his diary for 11 August 1905, he wrote:

I have the possibility of settling down to live at Tamanrasset or anywhere else in the Hoggar. I could have a house and a garden and settle down there for good. This possibility even seems to me like my Beloved's will.

I choose Tamanrasset, a village of twenty house-holds right in the mountains, in the heart of the Hoggar and the Dag Rali, who are its principal tribe. It is far from any of the important centres. It's unlikely it will ever have a garrison, tele-graph lines or a European presence, and there will not be a mission here for a long time. I'm choosing this forsaken spot and I'm settling here, imploring Jesus to bless this endeavour where I want my life to have as its sole model his life at Nazareth.

May he in his love deign to convert me, make me the way he wants me to be, make me love him with all my heart. Let me love him, obey

him and imitate him as much as I can at every
instant of my life. Sacred Heart of Jesus, your
Kingdom come.

Carnet de Tamanraset, p. 48

To his cousin Marie, he gave some details on the construction of his hermitage and told her about his projects:

My house is getting built: two rooms, each 1.75
metres wide and 2.75 long, about 2 metres high.
The walls are earth and stone. It will be finished
in 5 or 6 days. Afterwards we'll build a reed hut
to use as parlour, dining room, kitchen, bedroom
for Paul, guest rooms. For the security of the
Blessed Sacrament, I'll sleep beside it.
I picture myself leading the life of Nazareth here
for an indefinite time. Paul will work in the gar-
den with me and I'll make wooden platters. I'll
try to do a little good to the people around me
and pray to our one Beloved.

Letter to M. de Bondy, 26 August 1905

As soon as he had come into contact with the Tuaregs
in their country, he had started studying their language
and undertaken to compile a dictionary. He was also
preparing a translation of the Gospels and some passages
from the Wisdom Books of the Old Testament which
seemed specially appropriate.

The time I don't spend walking or resting I use
to prepare the ways. I try to make friends with

the Tuaregs, and I make lexicons and translations that those who come here to bring Jesus will absolutely need.

Letter to Fr. Huvelin, 13 July 1905

I divide my time between prayer, relations with the local people and my work on the Tuareg language. I give this last thing a big place. First, I'd like to get it over and done with and be altogether free for the other things. And besides, I need this language work. I can't do the Tuaregs any good except by speaking with them and knowing their language.

Letter to Fr. Huvelin, 4 December 1909

In fact, the language was not all that Brother Charles studied. He took an interest in the people's culture and started paying attention to all its elements. Over the years he transcribed the poems people sang in the evening around the fire, and which transmitted the tribe's history and soul. It was three days before his death that he noted: *"finished the translation of the collection of Tuareg poems."*

Approachachable and Unimposing

Remaining by himself in the Hoggar meant, by the liturgical rules of the times, that Brother Charles had to give up celebrating the Eucharist as long as there were no other Christians with him. His bishop asked him about this and he answered:

> *You ask me if it's better to live in the Hoggar without being able to celebrate the Holy Mass or to celebrate Mass but not live there. I've often asked myself the same thing. I used to incline always to sacrifice everything else to the celebration of Holy Mass. But there must be something wrong with this line of reasoning. Since the Apostles, the greatest saints have sometimes sacrificed their possibility of celebrating Mass to works of spiritual charity.*
> *Living alone in a place is a good thing. You achieve something even if you don't do much, because you start to belong to the country. You're approachable and unimposing there: it gives you such "littleness."*
>
> Letter to Bishop Guérin, 2 July 1907

This is not to say that his choice didn't cost him deeply. Besides, the adaptation was hard. Brother Charles suffered from isolation and went through a time of depression. Prayer had become a real struggle:

> *I'm not pleased with myself. I'm lax and cold. My prayers are extremely lukewarm, I've no mortification, my life is banal, passionless and empty. Prayer is difficult for me. As soon as I start, I'm attacked by sleep or by unbearable*

thoughts. This difficulty comes no matter what time I try to pray.

Am I wrong to distract myself like this? Would it be better to go on with my exercises of piety and not cut a minute off them, just asking God to help me?

Letter to Fr. Huvelin, 15 July 1906

He had hopes of getting a companion in 1907, but the man fell sick and had to turn around before he even got to the Hoggar.

His life seemed like a failure to him:

You know my wretchedness. You know how much I need you to pray for me. Over 21 years ago you brought me back to Jesus. What a harvest I should have by now, for myself and for others. And instead of that, I have wretchedness and bankruptcy for myself, and not the least good for others. A tree can be told by its fruits, and mine show what I am.

Letter to Fr. Huvelin, 1 January 1908

The Hoggar was in the grip of a terrible drought:

This year has been hard for the country. It hasn't rained for 17 months. That means raging famine in a country that lives on its milk, and where the poor have almost nothing else than milk to live on. The goats are as dry as the earth is, and the

people as dry as the goats.
Letter to M. de Bondy, 17 July 1907

He shared his reserves to the bottom of his stock. Finally he reached a state of exhaustion himself, and fell sick after one Christmas when he had felt himself very alone.

Christmas. No Mass tonight, for the first Christmas in 21 years. May my Beloved's will be done. In his mercy he's still let me have the Blessed Sacrament here. Up till the last minute I had hoped that someone would come, but nothing happened. No Christian traveller or soldier came, and I didn't get my permission to celebrate Mass alone. It's been three months, more than three months since I got any letters.
Letter to M. de Bondy, 25 December 1907

I've been rather sick these past days. I don't know just what it is, something wrong with my heart, I think. I'm not coughing, no chest pains, but the slightest movement leaves me so out of breath I could almost faint. A day or two ago I thought I might be going to die.
Letter to M. de Bondy, 26 January 1908

This time he was the one who was poor, in his state of debility and sickness. Up until then he had been trying to be approachable and unimposing, but he was still the one doing the giving, aiding others when they were in distress. Now he was the one who needed them, and it was the Tuaregs who would save him, giving him their most precious possession in that time of famine:

> *The people went around to all the goats for a radius of 4 km to get me a little milk.*
>> Letter to M. de Bondy, January 1908

He had had to be reduced to an extreme state of need, and then the Tuaregs had been able to give him something. The reversal in their situations was to be the ground from which genuine friendships could spring up and grow between Brother Charles and the Tuaregs. Friendship needs reciprocity and sharing.

> *The Tuaregs around here treat me with growing trust. Those I was already friends with are now closer, and new friendships are forming. I do them what services I can. I try to show them my love. When it seems like a favourable occasion, I speak about natural religion, about God's commandments, his Love, how to live in harmony with his Will, loving one's neighbour, and so on.*
>> Letter to Fr. Voillard, 12 Janurary 1912

The Apostolate of Friendship

In 1909, he wrote:

Brother Charles with the young Ouksem at Tamanrasset.

My apostolate should be one of goodness. When people see me they should say: "If this man is good, his religion must be good."

If someone asks me why I am mild and good, I should say: "Because I am the servant of someone much better than I am. If you only knew how good my master Jesus is." I want to be good enough that people will say: "If this is what the servant is like, what must the master be?"

Carnet de Tamanrasset, pp. 188-189

At a time when it was not rare to hear people say simplistically, "Outside the Church, no salvation," he confided to a Protestant friend:

I am not here to convert the Tuaregs all at once, but to try to understand them. I am sure that God will welcome those who have been good and upright into heaven. You are a Protestant, T. is an agnostic, the Tuaregs are Muslims. I'm convinced that God will receive us all if we have deserved it.

Quoted by Lehureaux in Au Sahara avec le Père de Foucauld, p. 115*

Since he had got to the Hoggar, he had always known that there was no question of looking for converts:

* Some quote this conversation by adding, after 'in heaven': 'without their needing to be Roman Catholics'. Exactly what Charles de Foucauld said in these refuted words remains uncertain.

> *I'm not to talk to them directly about Our Lord.*
> *That would just make them go away. I'm to gain*
> *their confidence, make friends with them, do*
> *them little services, deepen a friendship between*
> *us and encourage them discreetly to abide by*
> *natural religion.*
>
> Letter to M. de Bondy, 16 December 1905

But deep in his heart he kept a boundless desire that
the people might one day know that God was their
Father and that Jesus had died for them:

> *Will it be given to the generations that come*
> *after us to see the multitudes of North Africa say*
> *together, "Our Father who are in Heaven, hal-*
> *lowed be your name, your kingdom come, your*
> *will be done on earth as in heaven," and*
> *address God as the Father of all humanity,*
> *knowing that they are all brothers and sisters in*
> *him, loving their neighbours as themselves? I*
> *do not know. It is the secret of God. But it is our*
> *duty to work towards it with all our strength. It*
> *is an application of the second commandment*
> *to love our neighbours as ourselves, so like the*
> *first commandment, to love God above all else.*
>
> Letter to H. de Castries, 10 December 1911

In 1910, he started building a second hermitage up in
the mountains on the Assekrem plateau about 60 km
from Tamanrasset:

I don't see many Tuaregs just now. They are all up in the mountains, in the area of the spot where I'm having my hermitage built and where in the future, I'll spend half the time I consecrate to the Tuaregs. Construction started on the hermitage a month ago and it should be finished by now. It's right in the heart of the Hoggar, in the most central point of the mountain range which forms the people's citadel. Their tents (that is, their women, children, and old people) always stay within it.

Letter to M. de Bondy, 16 June 1910

He spent several months there in 1911. The beauty of the panorama moved him:

The view is more beautiful than anyone can express or even imagine. Nothing can give you an idea of the forest of peaks and rocky spires I have at my feet. It is a marvel. You cannot see it without thinking of God. I have a hard time taking my eyes away from this wonderful view. The beauty of it and the impression of infinity it gives you bring you close to the Creator.

Letter to M. de Bondy, 9 July 1911

But what made him happiest was the possibility of deepened contacts with the Tuaregs:

I'm very pleased with my stay here. People come to see me every 4 or 5 days at least, even though

the camps are far from here at the moment because of the drought. Since my visitors come from a day, a day and a half, or two days away, they finish the day with me and sleep here. A meal or two in common, a day or a day and a half spent together, draw you closer than a large number of visits a half-hour or an hour long, as they are at Tamanrasset.
Letter to M. de Bondy, 15 August 1911

The years passed and Brother Charles became more and more involved in every aspect of the life of his Tuareg friends. In many little ways he sought to better their living conditions. During his last visit to France he asked his cousin to teach him to knit, and on 16 April 1915 he wrote to her:

The knitting and crocheting have worked out well. The women are learning both and quite a few young people are crocheting sweaters. We have run out of hooks and yarn. If you could send some of both and also send some cottonseed by Vilmorin you would be doing a great service for the country. These things are also useful spiritually because everything is connected. It is easier for them to understand material progress and through working concretely for it they become used to work. This in turn will help them have a more settled life, open their minds to other ways and make them desirous of wider travel. Materially they have already made great progress. When I first arrived here there were two tiny houses and fifty huts. Now there are eighty houses, including one very sturdy one with a hut attached. And it is thus in all areas of life...

Letter to M. de Bondy, 16 April 1915

Already in Nazareth Brother Charles had written a meditation on the words of Jesus after the raising of Jairus' daughter, "Give her something to eat":

Have that tender care that expresses itself in the little things that are like a balm for the heart...With our neighbours go into the smallest details, whether it is a question of health, of consolation, of prayerfulness, or of need. Console and ease the pain of others through the tiniest of attentions. Be as tender and attentive towards those whom God puts on our path, as a brother towards brother or as a mother for her child. As much as possible be an element of consolation for those around us, as soothing balm, as our Lord was towards all those who drew near to him.

He had written to Bishop Guérin: *"For the spreading of the Gospel I am ready to go to the end of the world and live till the last judgment."* [Letter to Bishop Guérin, 27 February 1903] The same desire that made him write that now burned higher and higher. Facing a task of this immense size, he was still alone. It was then that he foresaw with amazing intuition the importance of lay people for evangelisation. This triggered his final project: an association of lay people, the Union of Brothers and Sisters of the Sacred Heart of Jesus.

Charles wrote to one of the first members of this association, J. Hours, and set out what such evangelisation was to consist of in its fundamental lines. This is an important letter, for in it Brother Charles vigorously summed up his deepest conception of the meaning of mission, as the Gospel and his own experience gave him light to see it:

> *I have received your letter. You say things that are quite true about the need everywhere, in France as in mission countries, for the work of the Church to be backed up by the work of lay people. I have been thinking along these same lines for some time.*
>
> *As you say, the ecclesiastical world and the world of lay people have so little to do with each other that the clergy give the laity no chance. It is certain that working alongside priests there need to be Priscillas and Aquilas, * who can see*

* St. Paul met Aquila and his wife Priscilla at Corinth, where they had just arrived after being expelled from Rome (Acts 18:2). Paul considered them excellent collaborators and very dear friends. (Acts 18:18-19; Rm 16:3; 1 Co 16:19; 2 Tm 4:19)

what the priest does not see, go where the priest cannot go. They can reach those who escape the priest and evangelise them by a contact that does them good, by a kindness that overflows to all, a love always ready to give itself, a good example attracting those who turn their backs on the priest and are determined to be hostile to him.

I think the problem goes very deep. Basic virtues are missing, or else are not strong enough. Virtues fundamental to Christian life – like charity, humility, mildness – are shallow and misunderstood.

Charity, which is the heart of religion (our first duty is to love God; our second, which is like the first, is to love our neighbour as ourselves) obliges all Christians to love their neighbour, meaning every human being, as themselves and consequently to make their neighbour's salvation, like their own, the great aim of their lives.

Every Christian must therefore be an apostle. This is not a counsel, it is a commandment, the commandment of charity.

To be an apostle, how? By the means God puts at each person's disposal. Priests have their superiors who tell them what they should do. Lay people must be apostles towards all those they can reach: their relations and their friends first of all, but not only these. There is nothing narrow about charity, its scope is as wide as the dimensions of the heart of Jesus. How to be an apostle? By the best means available, according to who it is the apostles are trying to reach. With anyone they are in touch with, making no exceptions, they must work by goodness, kindness, friendliness, the example of virtue, by humility and mildness, always such attractive and such Christian attitudes. With some people they should never say a word about God or religion, but wait patiently as God waits patiently, be good as God is good, show respectful affection and pray. With others they should speak of God to the extent that these are ready for it, and as soon as they reach the point of wanting to seek the truth by studying religion, they can put them in touch with a well-chosen priest who will know how to do them good.

Above all, apostles must see every human being as their brother or sister: "You are all brothers and sisters since you have only one Father, and he is in heaven." They must see every human being as a child of God, a soul redeemed by the blood of Jesus, a soul Jesus loves, a soul we must love as we love ourselves and whose salvation we must work for.

We must banish any spirit of triumphalism. "I am sending you out like sheep among wolves," Jesus said. How far from Jesus' way of speaking and acting is the triumphalist spirit of some who are not Christians, or who are bad ones, and who see enemies to combat where they should see ailing brothers and sisters to care for, wounded victims lying on the path for whom they should be good Samaritans.

It would appear that parents in the home, priests at their catechism lessons and all whose mission it is to rear children and train the young, should instil these truths in them from their earliest years and keep coming back to them:

— Every Christian must be an apostle. It is an obligatory duty of charity.

— Every Christian must see each human being as a beloved brother or sister. A sinner, an enemy of God, the Christian must see as someone ill, very ill, and should feel a deep pity and should care for that person as for a wayward brother or sister. Non-Christians may have a Christian for their enemy; the Christian must always be a loving friend towards every person and have towards them all the same feelings as Jesus has in his Heart.

— Be charitable, mild and humble towards all people. This is what Jesus taught us to do. Do not set out to conquer anybody. Jesus taught us to go "like lambs among wolves" and not to speak roughly or spitefully, not to throw insults, not to take up arms.

— Make themselves all things to all people in order to give Jesus to them all. Do it by having kindness and friendliness towards everyone, by rendering them all possible services, by contacts with them that show affection, by caring about

them all and treating them as brothers and sisters. And thus, lead souls gradually to Jesus by putting into practice Jesus' goodness.

– Read the Holy Gospels over and over continually in order to have Jesus' actions, words and thoughts constantly in mind. In this way, come to think, speak, and act as Jesus would, and not by the examples and modes of the world, whose practices we quickly fall back into if we take our eyes away from our Divine Model.

This is the remedy, in my opinion. To apply it is difficult because it touches very basic things, the inner realities of the soul, and because the need for it is universal. But difficulty is not there to make us stop trying. The greater the difficulty, the more we must rather set to work rapidly and strive with all our might. God always helps those who want to serve him. Never has God failed his creatures. It is we creatures who fail God so often. Even if we are doomed not to succeed, we should work with no less ardour, for when we work for this cause we are doing nothing else than obeying God and accomplishing his will as he has made it known to us.

Letter to J. Hours, 3 May 1912

V

IN THE LIKENESS OF JESUS
EVEN UNTO DEATH

The Means Jesus Used

The years went by, and Brother Charles could feel his physical strength diminishing. He wrote to his cousin:

> *Don't worry. I don't have the strength any more to kill myself working. When I do just a little bit more than my limit, I feel it straight away and I slow down. I put all I can into it, but it's far from being as much as I used to do. Besides, I'm so often interrupted by visits that I have plenty of unplanned relaxations.*
>
> Letter to M. de Bondy, 17 March 1914

He kept on going and felt deep peace about it:

> *I cannot say that I desire death. I used to desire it, but now I see so much good to be done, so many souls without a shepherd, that what I most want is to do a little good and work a little for*

the salvation of those poor souls. Still, God loves them far more than I do and doesn't need me. May his will be done.

There's nothing really wrong with me, but the summer wears me down. I get feverish spells sometimes, headaches, sleepless nights. Nothing that lasts and nothing severe. It will go away when the hot weather does, in five weeks. I'm leading my usual life, but getting less work done.

Letter to M. de Bondy, 20 July 1914

In this final stage of his life, Brother Charles seems to have surrendered himself more and more into God's hands: *"His will be done."* He made Jesus' prayer at Gethsemane his own, the prayer of total self-surrender to love:

"We are to love God, then, because he loved us first." [1 Jn 4:19] The Passion on Calvary is a supreme declaration of love. It was to redeem us that you suffered so much, O Jesus. The least of your acts has infinite worth, since it is one of God's acts, and would have been more than ample enough to redeem a thousand worlds, to redeem all possible worlds. But you suffered so much because you wanted to make us holy, to bear our burdens and to draw us into loving you freely. Loving is the most powerful way to attract love, loving is the most powerful way to make oneself loved.

It is impossible for us to love him and not imitate him, to love him and not want to be the way he was, do what he did, suffer and die in torment because he suffered and died in torment. It is impossible to love him and want to be crowned with roses when he was crowned with thorns. We must love him as he has loved us.

La Bonté de Dieu, p. 194

In 1900 Brother Charles had written to Fr. Huvelin from Nazareth:

My life goes on exactly the same way. It is more and more secluded and silent, more and more hidden and lost to view. I am delighted to see myself becoming invisible.

Letter to Fr. Huvelin 8 February 1900

It may be that he still took a little satisfaction in his solitary "seclusion" at Nazareth.

Now Brother Charles was linked by deep bonds to the Tuareg people. He had waited in vain to have followers, he was growing old, and he felt like a tree with no fruit. *"Unless a wheat grain falls on the ground and dies, it remains only a single grain. But if it dies, it yields a rich harvest."* [Jn 12:24]

To be a saviour with Jesus, we have to pass as he did through suffering, apparent failure and death:

The means Jesus used at his birth in the Manger, at Nazareth and on the Cross are these: poverty, utter lowliness, humiliation, rejection, persecution, suffering, the cross. These are our arms, the ones used by our divine Bridegroom, who asks us to let him continue his life in us. Let us follow him as our sole model and we are sure to do much good, for in that case it will not be we who live but he who lives in us. Our acts will no longer be our own, human and frail, but his divinely efficacious acts.

Letter to Bishop Guérin, 15 January 1908

The War Years

On 3 August 1914, war broke out between France and Germany. Brother Charles did not hear it until a month later, and the news rocked him. What ought he to do?

Soon afterwards, on 15 September, he wrote to his cousin:

You'll sense how deeply it costs me to be so far from our soldiers and the front. But my duty obviously is to stay here.

Letter to M. de Bondy, 15 September 1914

However, he was tormented by the thought of his comrades in combat. In December he wrote to his friend General Laperrine:

Wouldn't I be more useful at the front as a chaplain or stretcher bearer? If you don't write me to come I will stay here peacefully, but if you say come I will leave immediately and make haste.
Letter to Laperrine, 14 December 1914

Laperrine's answer came two months later: *"Stay where you are."*

The war moved Charles deeply because it touched his own roots: his memory of the War of 1870, the city he had had to flee, his birthplace he had never seen again.

He wrote to G. Tourdes, his childhood friend:

My dear Gabriel,
How I think of you since the war began! How much I thought about you when I heard about the combats at St. Dié, the city falling and being taken back again. I worry about you, worry about your brother, worry about your nephew who is probably under fire. Please, please, send me news. We'll talk about all the rest when we see each other after the war is won. If, as I firmly hope, we come out the winners, we will make a trip together to visit Strasbourg as a French city again.
Lettre à un Ami de Lycée, 25 November 1914

Reading these letters and others which contain harsh judgments on the enemy, we feel Charles' whole being vibrating in tune with the wave of patriotism that was sweeping his country. He was a man of his time, rooted in a historical epoch and moulded by the human surroundings that produced him. This was the human clay that God had to work with.

Torn two ways by the situation, he chose in spite of everything to stay in the Hoggar, where the repercussions of the conflict were soon making themselves felt.

The French army reduced the number of troops stationed in Algeria, and a rebel movement started to develop. It was supported by Tripolitania (today's Libya) and other foreign powers. Armed raiding parties from Morocco also became more and more of a threat.

Brother Charles, alone at Tamanrasset, was in a very exposed position. The officers of the nearest garrison advised him to come and live there, but he declined. He wanted to stay with the handful of people who had accepted in 1905 to let him come and live with them, when others the year before had refused to let him stay.*

The passing years had brought deeper familiarity and mutual respect, and friendship had grown. And now in the hour of his friends' danger, Brother Charles, bonded to them by new solidarity, could not abandon them.

His death was to show that human bonds of mutual love are stronger than all the nationalisms that keep us apart. Moussa Ag Amastan, the Tuareg chieftain who had

* See Carnet de Beni Abbès, p. 150-1

118

Brother Charles and a Tuareg at Tamanrasset.

let Charles stay, wrote to Brother Charles' sister two weeks after Charles' death:

> *Much blessing descend on our friend Marie. As soon as I learnt of the death of our friend, your brother Charles, my eyes clouded over. All has become dark for me. I wept and shed many tears and I am in deep mourning. His death gives me greatest sorrow.*
>
> *...Greet on my behalf your daughters, your husband and all your friends and say to them: "Charles the Marabout has not died only for you. He has also died for us all. May God grant him mercy and may we all be together with him in Paradise."*

Quoted by R. Bazin, *Charles de Foucauld*, p. 466

To Give One's Life out of Love

Brother Charles had long wanted to die a martyr.

At the monastery of Akbes in 1896, he had witnessed the horrible massacre of the Armenians by the Turks, and had suffered because he felt his nationality was protecting him.

He had written at that time to his cousin:

> *All over Armenia, and quite close to us too, there have been terrible massacres. But we were never in any real danger, I think. Because we're Europeans, the Turkish government takes great*

precautions to keep anything from happening to us. But for the Armenians it was horrible; people speak of 100,000 killed.

Letter to M. de Bondy, 19 February 1896

At the end of March, we at Akbes and all the Christians for two days around ought to have been dead. I was not found worthy. That is justified a thousand times, but what a sorrow I feel. Pray for me that I be converted and that God will not refuse me the next time.

Letter to M. de Bondy 24 June 1896

He perhaps was remembering scenes of this massacre when he wrote from Nazareth on 6 June 1897:

Picture yourself dying a martyr, stripped of everything, stretched out on the ground, naked, unrecognisable, covered with blood and with wounds, violently and painfully slain – and desire it to happen today.

Voyageur dans la nuit, p. 35

At Beni Abbès he noted:

Prepare constantly for martyrdom and receive it without a shadow of self-defence, as did the Lamb of God. Receive martyrdom in Jesus, through Jesus, like Jesus and for Jesus.

Seul avec Dieu, p. 103

At Tamanrasset, he wrote again in a prayer:

> *My Lord Jesus, you said, "There is no greater love than to lay down one's life for one's friends." With all my heart I want to give my life for you, I beg it of you earnestly. Nevertheless, not my will but yours be done. I offer you my life, do with me whatever you want most. My God, forgive my enemies and bring them to salvation.*
>
> *Voyageur dans la nuit, pp. 177-1898*

In 1916, the insecurity got worse. Tamanrasset was threatened both by raiding parties from Morocco and by the Tuareg tribes that had joined the rebellion.

These threats led Brother Charles to come up with a new plan. He told Laperrine his reasons for it:

> *This is to announce to you my change of residence. I've even moved to a new neighbourhood. After living on the left bank of the Wadi Tamanrasset for 11 years in the hermitage you're familiar with, I've shifted to the right bank, on the little plateau on the north side and near the big tree. Here's why: about a year and a half ago when I could see the Moroccan bandits getting closer and closer to the Hoggar, I thought of building a little refuge here, a tiny Casbah. That way the population of Tamanrasset could take shelter in case the Moroccan raiders came here.*

I thought it over and asked the Dag Rali, my neighbours, their opinion. I saw they liked the idea and so I spoke to Saint-Léger and de la Roche about it and then made up my mind. I started

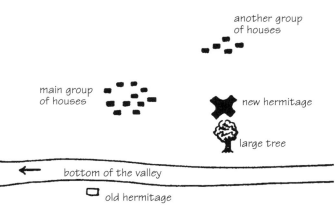

another group of houses

main group of houses

new hermitage

large tree

bottom of the valley

old hermitage

building it about a year ago, a very small affair, with just one workman helping me, a Haratin from the village. I picked the place for it with Ouksem. It's approximately on the highest point where the right bank of the riverbed rises up to the plateau, 150 metres from the big tree. It's a square enclosure with a courtyard 14 metres on a side and a turret at each corner. The walls are solid: a metre thick in good solid bricks.

As the construction was progressing, my Tuareg neighbours talked me into living there. They said that for one thing I would be nearer to them, and that, for another, if ever they had to take refuge there, it would be nicer to find someone

living there and the place stocked with provisions and tools. I finally let myself be persuaded and put up some rooms on the inside for myself to live in. The space of the courtyard is not significantly reduced and it's still large enough to receive the whole population of the village, including the nearby nomads. I moved in a week ago, even though construction is not quite terminated, because in order to finish it I needed the rafters, doors and windows from my old hermitage.
Letter to H. Laperrine, 1 July 1916

As we see, it was with his neighbours that Brother Charles made his decision about it all and on their request, "so that he could be nearer to them," that he moved in to live there.

Some soldiers from the nearest French outpost had stored arms in this refuge. They were to be distributed to thirty or so Tuaregs in charge of protecting Tamanrasset. Were the arms still there on 1 December? This is a disputed question.

For Brother Charles' part, his motivation is clear. He had built the "bordj", as his construction was called, to offer shelter to a population of poor and defenceless people with whom he felt in solidarity.

There is one case when we must resist evil forcefully. It is when it is not a case of defending ourselves but of protecting others. It takes forcefulness to defend the weak and the innocent when

124

their oppressors wrong them. The spirit of peace
is not a spirit of weakness but a spirit of strength.

Aux Plus Petits de Mes Frères, p. 131-2

On the other hand, when he alone was the one in danger, he wanted to imitate Jesus who met his violent death non-violently.

> *Let us be mild and gentle as the Lamb of God,*
> *without weapons to attack or weapons to defend*
> *ourselves. We are to let ourselves be bound,*
> *shorn, slaughtered, without resisting and with-*
> *out a word of protest.*
>
> *L'Imitation du Bien-aimé* p. 146

Undoubtedly it was because he had contemplated the Lamb of God, the lamb of Isaiah 53 that never opened his mouth, that he wrote in his rule for the Little Brothers of the Sacred Heart:

> *The little brothers are to call to mind each day*
> *that one of the gifts their Bridegroom Jesus has*
> *graciously bestowed on them is the possibility*
> *and the real hope that they may end their lives as*
> *martyrs. They are to prepare themselves con-*
> *stantly for this blessed end. They are to act at*
> *every moment as befits men who are called by*
> *the goodness of the Bridegroom to receive this*
> *infinite favour, and perhaps to receive it soon.*
> *They are to call down with their desires and their*

One of the last photographs of Brother Charles.

The seed that fell to the ground so silently the evening of 1 December 1916 has borne fruit.

When Brother Charles died, there were about forty lay people who formed the Union of Brothers and Sisters of the Sacred Heart of Jesus. He had founded this group several years before. One of the members, Louis Massignon, felt responsible for sharing Charles de Foucauld's spirituality and asked René Bazin to write a biography to make him known to a wider audience. This publication quickly resulted in drawing many followers.

Today, the spiritual family of Charles de Foucauld counts no less than 18 distinct groups, priests, religious women and men, and secular institutes. Through his writings and especially through the vitality of his life, many lay people recognized a Gospel life-style that also inspired them to gather as communities for their mutual support and encouragement. In addition, there are large numbers of individuals throughout the world who find nourishment in the spirituality of Charles de Foucauld without any formal affiliation to these groups.

They are attracted by the dynamism and relevance of his message for today's world. Due to his own temperament and religious formation, Charles de Foucauld felt a need to write a rule and precisely lay out a structure for the life which he envisioned. He took his commitment to his vocation as he understood it very seriously.

Despite all of this, he never allowed himself to be boxed in by rigid rules or a caricature of the life of

Nazareth. His reference point in living out his intuitions was always the living person of Jesus of Nazareth. The words and deeds of Jesus challenged him throughout the course of his life. He allowed the living Spirit of Jesus, which blows how it wills, to constantly direct him in the concrete situations in which he found himself.

A lively faithfulness to his fundamental intuition about Nazareth forged in him a keen attentiveness to the signs of his times and sensitized him to the suffering of others especially of the 'excluded'.

Brother Charles' witness remains a challenge to us today. Will we allow the Gospel to constantly speak to us in the midst of the situations in which we live, as it did for him? Will we allow the Gospel to shape our entire life and way of being?

It is this word which "does not return void, without accomplishing the work for which it was sent" (Is 53: 10-11) that is able to make our presence in the world a fruitful presence.

BIBLIOGRAPHY

Charles de Foucauld did not write any books, but he did write many personal 'meditations' and many 'letters' to family and friends. These, naturally, are in French, and relatively few, so far, have been translated into English.

For those who can read French, most of these 'spiritual writings' have been published (in 16 volumes) by Nouvelle Cité (from 1973 to 1997). The 'correspondence' with this or that person is published by a variety of publishers (Cerf, Seuil, Grasset etc.).

The following collections of 'meditations' and 'letters' are available in English:

Meditations of a Hermit, London: Burns & Oates, 1930 New York: Orbis Books, 1930

Sermons in the Sahara, London: Burns & Oates, 1938

Spiritual Autobiography of Charles de Foucauld, Jean-François Six, New Jersey: Dimension, 1964

A Little Brother of Jesus, Silent Pilgrimage to God, London: Darton, Longman and Todd, 1974,

Letters from the Desert, London: Burns & Oates, 1977

Spiritual Meditations on FAITH, New York: New City Press, 1988

Spiritual Meditations on HOPE, New York: New City Press, 1990

Come, sing a Song of Love Unknown, Prayers of Charles de Foucauld, New Jersey: Dimension, no date given.
Fifteen Days of Prayer with Charles de Foucauld, Michel Lafont, Missouri: Liguori Press, 1995
Charles de Foucauld: Selected Writings, Robert Ellsberg, New York: Orbis, 1999

There are also several biographies, including the following:

Rene Bazin, *Charles de Foucauld Hermit and Explorer*, London: Burns Oates, 1923 [The French original, 1921, made Charles de Foucauld known, but it is now definitely dated]

George Gorree, *Memories of Charles de Foucauld*, London: Burns Oates, 1938 [French original, 1936]

Anne Fremantle, *Desert Calling*, London: Hollis & Carter, 1950, [The first biography in English: well researched & reliable]

Michel Carrouges, *Soldier of the Spirit, the life of Charles de Foucauld*, Victor Gollancz, 1956

Margaret Trouncer, *Charles de Foucauld*, London: Harrap, 1972

Elizabeth Hamilton, *The Desert My Dwelling Place*, London: Hodder & Stoughton, 1968. [The best biography in English].

Charles Lepetit, *Two Dancers in the Desert*, New York: Orbis, 1983

Philip Hillyer, *Charles de Foucauld*, Collegeville, Minnesota: Liturgical Press, 1990 [Christian Mystics series]

Jean-Jacques Antier, *Charles de Foucauld*, San Francisco: Ignatius Press, 1999 [French original, 1997]

Ali Merad, *Christian Hermit in an Islamic World*, Paulist Press: New Jersey, 1999 [French original, 1975. This is a Muslim's view of Charles de Foucauld, of special interest today, as the translator, Zoe Hersov, shows in her foreword & postcript]

Charles de Foucauld, Catholic Truth Society: London, 2000. This is a small booklet in the CTS 'Biographies' Series.

Other writings concerning the Gospel way of Brother Charles include writings by: René Voillaume, Carlo Carretto, Emmanuel Asi, and Little Sister Magdeleine of Jesus.

SOME DATES

15 September 1858	Born at Strasbourg
30 October 1876	Enters military school
June 1881	Campaign against Bou Amana (South Oran District)
March 1882	Resigns from the army
10 June 1883	Begins exploration of Morocco
29 or 30 October 1886	Conversion
16 January 1890	Enters monastery of Our Lady of the Snows
11 July 1890	Arrives at the monastery of Akbes
23 January 1897	Receives permission from Abbot General to leave the Trappist Order
10 March 1897	Taken on as servant to the Poor Clares of Nazareth
9 June 1901	Ordained a priest
28 October 1901	Arrives at Beni-Abbès (South Oran District)
11 August 1905	Settles at Tamanrasset (Hoggar)
1 December 1916	Dies at Tamanrasset

TRANSLATION OF BROTHER CHARLES' LETTER TO FR HUVELIN

13 July 1905
About 20° North, near Timiaouin

Very dear Father,

For the first time in a long while I have a chance to get a letter to you. I think of you very often; your child, though such an unworthy one, is very faithful to you.

I'm not forgetting your feast day. Day after tomorrow, on St. Henry's Day, my poor prayer will be with you even more than usual. Happy Feast Day, beloved father. May the will of JESUS be done in you completely. This is the deep wish, the only wish, I offer you, and it is my prayer for you.

My trip is coming to an end well. I see a good number of local people. The one problem is myself: I am pleased with everything except myself.

Besides my countless shortcomings, there is one thing that bothers me: I wish I could recite the Breviary, have my hours of prayer and meditation and read my little passages of Holy Scripture at least somewhat the way I do when I'm stationary somewhere. And if I try to do it, I have no time left to chat with the Tuaregs or study their language to prepare the way as much as possible for those who will come after me. Since I'm not able to combine the two things, I let the first one go and do only the second, which seems to me the thing God wants most. Even though I think I am doing the right thing, this life without much time devoted exclusively to prayer, this neglect of the pious exercises that do me good and build up my strength, bothers me. I often ask myself if the impossibility of combining the two things is a real one or if it's the result of my lukewarmness.

Thanks be to JESUS, I've been able to celebrate Holy Mass nearly every day. But since I left Beni Abbès, I've almost always replaced the Breviary with the Rosary, and sometimes, putting off the Rosary till the evening, I didn't get through all fifteen decades. When we are on the march, I think about JESUS as much as I can, but sad to say I do it very poorly. When I'm not moving or resting, my time is spent preparing the ways, trying to make friends with the Tuareg and working on the dictionary and translations that will be essential for those who come here to bring JESUS. If I'm wrong to go about it like this, if I should leave off and do it some other way, tell me so and I will obey. In spite of my regrets at being so busy with exterior things, I think – until you tell me to do otherwise – that I am doing the right thing.

As to the future, I need your advice. The people will accept me. But I do not feel they will accept others. As long as no other priests are accepted among the Tuaregs, should I try to settle here, to stay here for a good part of each year? The more I think about it, the more the answer seems to be *yes*. Somebody has to keep this door open until others can come in by it. Someone has to make friends, build up trust, give a good impression, prepare the ground until the workers get here to till the field. It seems to me more and more that since JESUS, by your guidance, sent me here, I should keep trying to do his work till others get here to replace me.

The little group I'm travelling with will go back to In Salah towards the end of October. Should I go back then to Beni Abbès and not leave it ever again? Should I, on the contrary, settle permanently with the Tuaregs and not leave? Or should I divide my time between Beni Abbès and the Tuaregs until someone comes to replace me in one place or another? I'm inclined to choose the third thing, in spite of the disadvantages to it. For one thing, it makes my life so exterior, and for another thing, there's a question of money. Try to get word to me which of the three choices I should take. You will be obeyed.

Presently I'm trying to build a little house with the Tuaregs. It won't be the beginnings of a fraternity of the Sacred HEART as at Beni Abbès, just a simple shack I can live in. I won't have any land around, neither a lot nor a little; I won't try to cultivate anything. I'll just lead my life of prayer and make ropes and wooden bowls a good part of the year. I'll depend as little as possible on the land.

It's nearly nightfall. Farewell, beloved father. I kneel at your feet and beg you to bless your unworthy child, who loves you and reveres you faithfully with all his heart, in the HEART of our Beloved JESUS,

Br. Ch. of Jesus

Made in the USA
Charleston, SC
05 January 2011